THE NATIONAL INSTITUTE OF ECONOMIC AND SOCIAL RESEARCH

Occasional Papers
XXVII

RECENT TRENDS IN MONOPOLY IN GREAT BRITAIN

GH00586702

RECENT TRENDS IN MONOPOLY
IN GREAT BRITAIN

G. WALSHE

CAMBRIDGE UNIVERSITY PRESS

Published by the Syndics of the Cambridge University Press
Bentley House, 200 Euston Road, London NW1 2DB
American Branch: 32 East 57th Street, New York, N.Y.10022

© The National Institute of Economic and Social Research 1974

Library of Congress Catalogue Card Number: 74–76570
ISBN: 0 521 09863 7

First published 1974

Printed in Great Britain
at the University Printing House, Cambridge
(Brooke Crutchley, University Printer)

CONTENTS

TABLES

SYMBOLS AND CONVENTIONS

—   means nil or negligible

..   means not available

n.a.   means not applicable

Items may not always add to totals because of rounding.

PREFACE

The problems created by monopolies and mergers have raised important issues in public policy on industrial structure. It is now time to assess some aspects of monopoly in the United Kingdom which will impinge upon this policy in the future. First, it is necessary to know to what extent monopolisation persists over time; secondly, it is of fundamental importance to know whether monopolisation is promoted primarily by mergers and amalgamations, or by the rapid internal growth of one or two firms; thirdly, we need to know the extent of external constraints on the exercise of monopoly power.

The answers to these questions given here form part of a research project on mergers and business concentration directed by Professor P. E. Hart at the National Institute, which was assisted by grants from the Department of Employment and Productivity, and the Department of Trade and Industry. This book is a companion to a recent publication which examined the causes and consequences of changes in industrial concentration in the typical British industry in the period 1958–63;[1] the same case-study approach is used here on the highly monopolised industries. This paper also supplements the statistical framework provided by other work published from the research project.[2]

The completion of the research project must await the publication of concentration data from the 1968 Census of Production. The final stages of the research will blend the statistical and descriptive approaches in assessing the effects of mergers on concentration.

My work on this topic benefited considerably from discussions with my colleagues in the research team, P. E. Hart and M. A. Utton, and with other economists at the National Institute, in particular the Director, G. D. N. Worswick, and S. J. Prais and G. F. Ray. I should also like to

[1] P. E. Hart, M. A. Utton and G. Walshe, *Mergers and Concentration in British Industry*, Cambridge University Press, 1973.

[2] P. E. Hart, 'Concentration in the United Kingdom' in H. Arndt (ed.), *Die Konzentration in der Wirtschaft*, Berlin, Duncker and Humblot, 1971 and 'Entropy and other measures of concentration', *Journal of the Royal Statistical Society*, (Series A), vol. 134, part 1, 1971, pp. 73–85; M. A. Utton, 'The effect of mergers on concentration: U.K. manufacturing industry, 1954–65', *Journal of Industrial Economics*, vol. 20, 1971, pp. 42–58, 'Some features of the early merger movements in British manufacturing industry', *Business History*, vol. 14, 1972, pp. 51–60 and 'Mergers and the growth of large firms', *Bulletin of the Oxford University Institute of Economics and Statistics*, vol. 34, 1972, pp. 189–97.

thank Leslie Hannah of St John's College, Oxford for his comments on some of the draft chapters. Countless experts in firms, trade associations, ministries and research organisations have supported this research by providing information. This co-operation has been invaluable, but the list of names is too long to mention and, moreover, some confidences need protecting. I am also grateful to Mrs K. Jones and Miss G. I. Little for preparing this book for publication, and to Miss Carol Entwistle and Miss Janet Laraway for their efficient secretarial services. Finally, the usual caveat holds; the many people who have helped in this study are not responsible for any errors that remain in the work, they are the author's responsibility and his alone.

March 1973   G.W.

CHAPTER I

INTRODUCTION

THE AIMS OF THE STUDY

The basic purpose of this book is to provide information which will assist in the development of public policy towards monopoly in the United Kingdom. It traces the business histories of monopolised products to show whether internal or external expansion of firms has been used to obtain market power, provides data on the persistence of monopoly and of near-monopoly over time, and discusses the constraints on the exercise of monopoly power. Thus the aim is to summarise the ascertainable facts about the creation, maintenance and limits of monopoly power in the United Kingdom.

At least three important questions need to be answered if monopoly policy is to have a sensible frame of reference. The first is whether oligo-poly and monopoly positions have been achieved primarily by internal or by external growth of firms. If firms typically achieve market dominance through internal growth, a policy towards monopoly or oligopoly focused primarily on mergers would be misconceived in that it would be treating only a minor portion of the problem. On the other hand, if external growth was the typical route to market dominance, a procedure of vetting mergers would be sufficient to hinder the emergence of monopoly power.

There is no shortage of opinions on the advent of monopolies, but precise knowledge of the relative importance of internal and external growth is rather sparse. For example, Mennel thinks that the classical model of perfect competition no longer applies:

The model which reflects the real situation is one in which all the important sectors of the economy are dominated by fewer and fewer corporations; by a growth of monopoly which is the antithesis of competition . . . The take-over bids measured in millions and even hundreds of millions of pounds have drawn the attention of the general public to the process of the centralization of control in fewer and fewer hands.[1]

Again, the following extract from Bannock is typical of writings on the growth of large firms:

Advocates of the desirability of further mergers and concentration often meet objections at the elimination of the smaller and medium-sized companies by

[1] W. Mennel, *Takeover. The Growth of Monopoly in Britain, 1951–61*, London, Lawrence and Wishart, 1962, p. 9.

pointing to the fact that in Britain, Germany and the United States, the total number of registered companies or corporations continues to grow slowly, losses through liquidation and acquisition being more than compensated for by new company formations. However, this argument has little force in view of the established fact that this increasing number of companies accounts for a rapidly diminishing proportion of total business. Most of these surviving companies remain small or are acquired by much larger corporations, thus feeding the concentration of the economy at the top.[1]

But the only systematic account of the part that mergers have played in promoting monopoly and near-monopoly in the United Kingdom is still that made by Evely and Little, relating to a period ending over twenty years ago.[2] This is discussed in the next chapter.

The second important question concerning monopoly is its permanence. If, typically, monopoly positions are rapidly eroded, either by new entry or by the growth of firms which previously were small, then monopoly policy could be seen as treating a transient problem and its relevance could be questioned. Marxists usually offer an apocalyptic view of the durability of monopoly.[3] They foresee the collapse of the capitalist organisation of markets, all eventually dominated by monopolists, who will be swept away as the workers take over the consolidated enterprises and state monopoly is instituted. Other commentators such as Stigler predict the erosion of monopoly and oligopoly over time for quite different reasons.[4] In Stigler's model, monopolists operate in a world of low entry barriers and so long as they earn excessive profits new firms will be attracted into their industries. Worcester came to a similar conclusion vis à vis the 'dominant firm' where constant or decreasing returns to scale could be assumed.[5] With increasing returns to scale, however, either the competition of smaller firms would be accommodated in a collusive oligopoly, or the dominant firm would become a monopolist. Empirical studies of what has happened to monopolies and near-monopolies in the United Kingdom over the years are made in chapters 2 to 4.

The third question for discussion is whether monopolies and near-monopolies in the United Kingdom are constrained, and whether the magnitude of the problem is at all serious. The textbook vision of monopolists left free to determine a price and output policy without reference

---

[1] G. Bannock, *The Juggernauts*, London, Weidenfeld and Nicholson, 1971, p. 47.

[2] R. W. Evely and I. M. D. Little, *Concentration in British Industry*, Cambridge University Press, 1960, chap. VIII.

[3] See, for example, S. Aaronovitch, *Monopoly: a study of British monopoly capitalism*, London, Lawrence and Wishart, 1955, chap. I.

[4] G. J. Stigler, 'Monopoly and oligopoly by merger', *American Economic Review*, vol. 40, 1950, pp. 23–34.

[5] D. A. Worcester Jnr., 'Why "dominant" firms decline', *Journal of Political Economy*, vol. 65, 1957, pp. 338–46. Worcester's 'dominant firm' can be described as a near-monopolist who acts as a price leader for the product market.

to anything but the market demand curve is not very helpful in practice. For this reason we need to know, for example, whether import competition is significant, and whether countervailing power exercised by buyers of monopolised products can be said to safeguard consumers' interests. Again, if there really are only a few instances of non-trivial, unconstrained monopoly or tight oligopoly situations in British industry, it could be argued that the importance of the monopoly problem has been exaggerated. Examples of monopolies or oligopolies in the United Kingdom which might be deemed trivial are the duopoly in cricket-ball manufacture,[1] and the former monopoly in tuning forks.[2] No doubt there are numerous other instances of small-scale monopoly, duopoly and oligopoly in British industry, whether constrained or unconstrained, but they have not been included in the present study which is restricted to products with sales of at least £10 million in the 1963 Census of Production.[3]

DATA FROM THE CENSUS OF PRODUCTION

The uses and limitations of data from the Census of Production were discussed in the companion volume[4] and there is no need to traverse the same ground here. The measure of monopoly or near-monopoly power used is the concentration ratio, the share of United Kingdom sales of goods produced in the United Kingdom manufactured by a small number (usually five) of leading firms. Evely and Little used mainly three-firm concentration ratios, but in some cases they published ratios for four, five, or more firms.[5] Also, their information was in terms of employment, net output or gross output (the last approximately equal to sales).

The major limitations of concentration data of this kind are that imports are not counted as market supplies, that exports are not subtracted from home production to give a fair indication of home market power, and that they reveal nothing about vertical integration in an industry. Most important, the concentration ratio does not usually recognise close substitutes; products which compete in the same market place for the incomes of consumers may be treated as being in different categories, for example, wallpaper and paint. But the fact that the Census is arranged on a production rather than a market basis is not a fundamental deficiency provided that ordinary caution is exercised in interpreting results.

[1] Readers of Maidstone and Tonbridge Sports Industries.
[2] H. Townsend, 'Economic theory and the cutlery trades', *Economica*, vol. 21, 1954, p. 229. Pye of Cambridge now make an electronic, valve-maintained, tuning fork.
[3] Board of Trade, *Report on the Census of Production for 1963*, London, HMSO, 1969 (henceforth Census of Production 1963).
[4] Hart, Utton and Walshe, *Mergers and Concentration in British Industry*.
[5] *Concentration in British Industry*.

It is also possible that, even when the five-firm concentration ratio is high, the product market does not coincide with the generally accepted notion of a monopoly. A full discussion of what does and does not constitute a monopoly is not contemplated here, but it is quite reasonable to expect that a firm with a 70 per cent market share, or a duopoly with an 80 per cent market share, or a triopoly with a 90 per cent market share has some degree of monopoly or near-monopoly power, which can be exercised within constraints. It may be noted in passing that a precondition for Monopolies Commission investigations of single firms is whether the firm controls one quarter or more of market supplies (that is, production minus exports and plus imports). In the final analysis, the reader must judge for himself whether the criterion of a monopoly or near-monopoly situation used in this study (a five-firm sales concentration ratio of 90 per cent or more) is set too low or too high, and that judgement will have to wait until the case studies have been presented. Provisionally, the concentration ratio can be thought of as an indication of product areas where monopoly power is likely to exist, whereas the investigation which follows will demonstrate the accuracy or otherwise of this indication.

THE PLAN OF THE BOOK

The book commences with a glimpse of 'life at the top'. Chapter 2 traces the notable developments since 1951 in the high-concentration trades discussed by Evely and Little,[1] and attempts to judge whether, in those trades, high concentration has persisted over the ensuing twenty years or so. This in itself is an important datum for policy makers. But chapter 2 is also concerned with a major theme of the book in that it shows how the firms in the high-concentration trades chosen by Evely and Little obtained market dominance. To those unfamiliar with Evely and Little's work, therefore, chapter 2 acts as an introduction to their findings. It also attempts to eliminate a possible source of confusion: here we are concerned with the external and internal components of growth in market share; we examine the size of firms relative to others in a specific market and how the relative dominance of one or a few firms has been achieved. Thus a major preoccupation of chapter 2 will be to establish which of Evely and Little's trades were 'external-growth trades' and which were 'internal-growth trades'. This systematic search through the business histories of these trades should allow us to make a reliable judgement on the extent to which monopoly and near-monopoly has been durable over the period since 1951.

The 1963 Census of Production made it possible to study the emergence

---

[1] *Concentration in British Industry*, chaps. VIII and IX.

of monopoly power in a large number of product markets. The task of chapters 3 and 4 was considerably simplified by the procedures used in the Census to reduce the amount of published information to what were considered sensible proportions. Thus, very few product groups with sales of under £10 million in 1963 were given concentration ratios in the Census Summary.[1] Happily, a ready-made criterion of non-triviality was thus built into the data. A sales limit of £10 million was accepted here because it was thought that raising the limit, which it was possible to do with the data, would introduce unacceptable bias. Over half the products considered in chapters 3 and 4 had sales of under £30 million in 1963. There is no knowing what proportion of monopolies and near-monopolies were excluded by the limit of £10 million; clearly, there were numerous firms in a similar position to the two cricket-ball manufacturers. It is necessary, however, to keep sight of the monopolist as a dominant seller. The more small 'craft' monopolists were included in the distribution the less relevant the findings would be. In many cases of 'craft' monopoly it can be surmised that buyers are stronger than sellers. Again, if there are any important monopolies excluded by the limit, many are in declining or stagnant markets; sales of products in expanding markets will soon exceed £10 million. The Census also excluded certain heterogeneous product groups, thus leaving products which satisfied approximately the economic definition of a market.

In these chapters the selection of monopoly or near-monopoly is by *products* rather than by the *trades* of the 1951 Census. Because the 1963 Census publishes product concentration ratios, we are, in effect, studying market rather than industrial structures.[2] The former have been the traditional concern of the economic theory of the firm and of public policy on monopolies. The two chapters trace the emergence of monopoly or tight oligopoly in a total of thirty-two products, and particular attention is paid to the role of mergers in promoting high concentration.[3] The products surveyed in chapter 3 all had a five-firm sales concentration ratio for 1958 of 90 per cent or more according to the 1963 Census of Production. This level of concentration approximates to the concept of a highly monopolised product.

However, the Census published no concentration information for the eight products surveyed in chapter 4. These, which we call 'non-disclosure'

---

[1] Census of Production 1963, part 131, table 5.

[2] 'Trade' in the 1951 Census was more broadly defined than 'product' in the 1963 Census. The former included associated products and by-products which do not all compete in the same (or even similar) markets.

[3] Apart from Evely and Little's work, which is fully reviewed in chapter 2, the only other study of the part mergers have played in the emergence of high concentration is for the United States: J. F. Weston, *The Role of Mergers in the Growth of Large Firms*, Berkeley, University of California Press, 1952, chap. II.

products, are cases where a published concentration ratio might have revealed information relating to individual firms, which is expressly forbidden by the Statistics of Trade Act, 1947. It may be assumed that in each of these cases five-firm sales concentration was above 90 per cent. An unacceptable degree of bias would have affected the conclusions of this study had these products not been considered.

The findings of these two chapters are reconciled with those of Evely and Little in chapter 5.

Chapter 6 discusses briefly the nature of the constraints encountered by monopolists and near-monopolists in forty-four product markets. It is hoped that this will establish a correct perspective on the monopoly problem existing in the United Kingdom. The constraints on monopolists (as defined in this study) are competition from all other products, competition from imports, and potential competition from new entrants. Monopolists may be further constrained by large buyers of their products to the benefit of consumers; it is likely that they are also constrained by the existence of the Monopolies Commission.

This study has pursued the evidence of constraints upon monopolists with some degree of confidence that the facts were being uncovered. What cannot be revealed in a work of this kind is the prevalence of collusion between manufacturers, or the extent of covert restrictive practices by trade associations. Adam Smith's opinion is well known: 'People of the same trade seldom meet together, even for merriment and diversion, but the conversation ends in a conspiracy against the public, or in some contrivance to raise prices.'[1] Thus, it is as well to remind the reader that here the whole area of collusion has had to be ignored. Indeed, in some cases, patchy evidence about collusion in a specific trade has not been presented; the policy has been to say nothing where the evidence is unsystematic. Certainly one would like to know all the facts on collusion in all industries, but since our knowledge falls far short of this it is best to say nothing.

[1] *The Wealth of Nations* (ed. E. Cannan), London, Methuen, 1930, vol. I, book I, chap. x, part II, p. 130.

CHAPTER 2

EVELY AND LITTLE'S SAMPLE OF HIGH-CONCENTRATION TRADES

THE STUDY BY EVELY AND LITTLE

The first object of this chapter is to examine the high-concentration trades classified by Evely and Little,[1] in order to allocate them to categories of external or internal growth. The second task is to study the sample for 1951 to discover whether monopoly or near-monopoly has persisted over time.

Evely and Little allocated the trades of the 1951 Census to one of three concentration categories – low, medium or high.[2] The criterion of high concentration was that 67 per cent or more of the employment, net output or gross output was shared by the three largest business units in the trade. However, for twenty of the fifty trades in this high-concentration category, Evely and Little were unable to obtain three-firm concentration ratios and ratios for four or five (or more) firms were used instead. Table 2.1 is a reproduction of Evely and Little's original table.

With the use of data from the Census, certain attributes of the high-concentration group were described; then thirty-six of the fifty trades were considered in more detail.[3] These thirty-six are referred to here as Evely and Little's sample of high-concentration trades. In each case, the leading firms in the trade were identified and their business histories traced. The aim was to allocate trades to one of three categories – those where the leading firms had achieved market dominance by mergers or external expansion; those where the leading firms had obtained dominance by internal growth; and those where no useful generalisation could be made. That is, the third category contained firms with differing growth experiences. Evely and Little were not examining the contribution of external and internal growth to the total growth of the firm, rather they were estimating how relative market power in a trade had been achieved by the leading firm or firms. It is quite possible to find a case of a diversified firm, which has grown internally for the most part, but which achieved dominance by external growth in one or more of its trades. These would then be classified as trades in which high concentration was produced by external expansion even though the major part of the growth of this diversified firm was attributable to internal expansion.

---

[1] *Concentration in British Industry.*
[2] Ibid. chap. IV, table 1, p. 51.
[3] The remaining fourteen trades are listed and considered in appendix B below.

Table 2.1.   *High-concentration trades with employment or net output concentration ratios of 67 per cent and over in 1951*

	Total business units	Concentration ratios		Trade employment
		Employment	Net output	
		(percentages)		(000s)
Concentration ratios referring to more than 3 business units[a]				
Primary batteries (8)	8	100	100	9·0
Incandescent mantles (5)	5	100	100	0·8
Transmission chains (5)	5	100	100	6·1
Razors (excluding electric) (4)	11	94	99	3·9
Cotton thread (8)	27	94	91	12·7
Explosives and fireworks (6)	29	93	91	30·5
Asbestos cement goods (4)	9	92	92	7·3
Photographic plates and films (4)	14	90	91	10·2
Cement (4)	12	87	89	12·3
Accumulators and parts (4)	20	86	89	7·5
Motorcycles etc. (4)	17	86	87	15·0
Wallpaper (4)	16	86	86	5·5
Matches and firelighters (6)	27	85	86	4·1
Scales and weighing machinery (6)	23	85	83	6·0
Spirit distilling (6)	38	80	73	5·3
Margarine (4)	27	77	85	5·3
Iron and steel tubes (4)	81	77	79	42·4
Vinegar and other condiments (4)	21	75	80	1·9
Zinc (5)	42	68	82	8·1
Wholesale bottling of wines and spirits (7)	112	58	74	9·2
Concentration ratios referring to the 3 largest business units				
Valves and cathode ray tubes	9	85	82	14·5
Mineral oil refining	8	84	85	12·1
Sugar and glucose	25	84	82	18·8
Salt mines, etc.	12	83	87	5·6
Precious metals refining	13	83	84	5·7
Starch	11	83	89	2·6
Small arms	15	82	85	5·2
Seed crushing and oil refining	26	81	79	9·4
Prime movers: internal combustion	25	77	80	28·3
Abrasive wheels etc.	19	76	79	5·4
Spirit rectifying	10	75	83	1·6
Tin	13	75	80	2·0
Floorcoverings	11	75	76	10·5
Tramways, trolleybuses, omnibuses	11	75	74	4·5
Rubber tyres and tubes	11	75	73	35·1
Ball and roller bearings	15	75	70	21·5
Fertilisers	68	73	75	16·5
Rayon, nylon yarn and staple fibres	10	72	82	40·3
Soap and glycerine	74	72	80	18·8

[a] Numbers of business units to which the concentration ratios refer given in brackets after the names of the trades.

Table 2.1. (cont.)

	Total business units	Concentration ratios		Trade employment
		Employment	Net output	
		(percentages)		(000s)
Tinplate	18	71	72	16·9
Tobacco	60	70	74	46·0
Cast iron stoves and grates (other)	15	68	69	9·9
Boilers and boilerhouse plant	40	67	62	26·5
Cast iron pipes and fittings	31	66	68	13·9
Notepaper, pads and envelopes	30	66	68	10·1
Ice cream	65	65	76	6·1
Asbestos manufactures	31	65	70	13·5
Bicycles and tricycles	99	64	69	26·4
Cinematograph film printing	18	61	70	2·4
Lead	40	53	69	3·2

SOURCE: Evely and Little, *Concentration in British Industry*, table 2.

Recognising that their approach was 'illustrative and not comprehensive', Evely and Little concluded: 'From the preceding discussion emerges the major importance of external expansion in the growth of the leading concerns in the highly concentrated trades. There are few firms indeed among the leaders in the trades surveyed which were not created by amalgamations or have not resorted to acquisition and merger at some stage during their development.'[1]

The merger history since 1951 of each trade in the sample is here examined to see if there is any significant break with the pattern of events before 1951. In addition, an attempt is made to eliminate the third category of cases where the leading firms had differing growth experiences. It would clearly be misleading to classify a trade as 'differing' if one firm with 80 per cent of the trade grew externally and another with 15 per cent grew internally. Thus, here, the growth experience of the dominant leading firm or firms will decide the issue. The yardstick, admittedly arbitrary, is 60 per cent or more of the trade. It is found that, in fact, only one trade, seed crushing and oil refining, cannot be given an un ambiguous classification.

At the beginning of this project an attempt was made to measure the durability of high concentration in all the fifty trades selected by Evely and Little by comparing the levels of concentration in 1951 with levels at a later date using the 1963 Census of Production. Unfortunately the data provided a very incomplete picture. Briefly, three of the fifty trades in 1951 have since been excluded from the Census, while for a further twenty-

[1] Ibid. p. 129.

three trades either aggregation with other trades, or dispersal among a number of other trades, prevented comparability. For twenty-four trades a limited comparison was possible, but unfortunately no conclusion could be drawn from the evidence in fifteen of these cases. Of the remaining nine trades it was possible to be reasonably confident that there were four increases in concentration, four decreases, and one where concentration was unchanged.

This result was felt to be inadequate and an alternative approach was adopted, which took the form of estimating the levels of concentration in the thirty-six trades for which Evely and Little prepared case studies, using all sources, official and unofficial. The limitations of this procedure are manifold, but two must be stressed here. First, the sources are not all equally reliable and, secondly, the estimates are not all for the same date owing to the variety of the sources. Where an informal estimate of the concentration level was the only solution, the various sources used are cited in footnotes. The results are summarised at the end of the chapter, by which time the reader should be sufficiently informed of the reliability or unreliability of the estimates to make his own judgement.

HIGH-CONCENTRATION TRADES WITH EXTERNALLY EXPANDED LEADING FIRMS

External growth occurs when:
    (a) many firms amalgamate, as it were, overnight;
    (b) two or three leading firms merge;
    (c) the leading firm(s) follows a policy of piecemeal acquisition over time.
Evely and Little placed the external-growth trades in these categories:
    (a) wallpaper, salt mines, cement, tobacco, lead, cast iron pipes, sugar and glucose, cotton thread;
    (b) matches and firelighters, transmission chains, explosives, incandescent mantles, zinc, tin, margarine;
    (c) spirit distilling, spirit rectifying, weighing machines, soap and glycerine, fertilisers, iron and steel tubes, tinplate, motorcycles, floor-coverings.
In addition one other trade, asbestos cement, classified by Evely and Little as expanding internally, has been reclassified as expanding externally and under category (b) (see page 16 below). Each of these categories is considered in turn.

Many-firm amalgamations

Of the eight trades in this group there were further mergers after 1951 in seven; only in cotton thread did no traceable merger activity occur.

In 1961 Wall Paper Manufacturers (WPM) acquired two companies which had had 20 per cent of the trade between them in 1960. Also Imperial Chemical Industries (ICI) entered the trade during 1960–1, by acquiring two companies which had roughly 4·5 per cent of sales in 1962.[1] Despite the tendency for WPM's share to fall over time in the absence of acquisitions, the 1961 acquisitions and ICI's internal growth on the basis of its initial acquisitions, increased the four-firm concentration ratio up to 1968. WPM's takeover by Reed International in 1965 consolidated the increase in concentration somewhat, as Reed produced 'ingrain' papers at the time. One estimate implies that WPM and ICI alone controlled just under 90 per cent of domestically produced output. This is consistent with information derived from trade sources for 1970–1, which indicates that the top four firms produced roughly 90 per cent of United Kingdom output. However, if account is taken of newer competing products not covered by the 1951 Census (vinyl wall-coverings), the top five firms control 84 per cent of sales.[2] The trade now resembles a duopoly, whereas before ICI's entry there was one dominant firm.

In salt, the acquisitions by Cerebos during the 1950s – the London Salt Company, and Palmer Mann with the 'Sifta' brand – meant that Cerebos dominated the domestic salt market. Cerebos was itself acquired by Ranks Hovis McDougall in 1968, but this did not affect the concentration ratio. Cerebos and Staveley Industries came to an agreement during the 1960s whereby their industrial and bulk salt interests were pooled in the British Salt Company, with Staveley having the majority interest (75 per cent). At least five salt works were closed down as a result of this step. The Cerebos acquisitions and the atrophy of all but one of the open-pan salt producers (Thompson Ingram) have increased the three-firm concentration by a few points. ICI, Cerebos and Staveley Industries controlled roughly 90 per cent of United Kingdom output by 1971.[3]

All three of the major firms in cement – Associated Portland Cement Manufacturers, Tunnel Cement and Rugby Portland Cement – made minor acquisitions during the 1960s. Associated Portland acquired a few works in 1966–7; Rugby acquired Eastwoods Cement in 1962 and Chinnor Industries in 1963; Tunnel acquired Caledonian Portland Cement in 1967. These were sufficient to increase four-firm concentration by a few

[1] For a fuller account of these events in this trade see Hart, Utton and Walshe, *Mergers and Concentration in British Industry*, pp. 130–4.

[2] Economist Intelligence Unit, *Retail Business*, no. 108, February 1967, p. 29.

[3] The 1951 Census excluded Northern Ireland, so that the small output of the rock salt mine at Carrickfergus is not included in this estimate, neither is the output of non-integrated establishments which separately process and pack salt – they were treated as miscellaneous foods in the 1951 Census. This left only Cerebos and the New Cheshire Salt Works in the domestic salt sector of the trade.

points up to the mid-1960s. Thereafter there was a tendency for small local firms to gain on the leading firms because of their transport cost advantages, but this was arrested by Associated Portland's investment in major new plants over the period 1969–71.[1]

The situation in tobacco is covered elsewhere.[2] Both Imperial Tobacco and Gallaher made acquisitions in the cigars and cigarettes markets after 1951. But internal growth of these two firms, and of Carreras, since import rationing ended in the mid-1950s, also helped to achieve at the very least a 15 per cent increase in three-firm concentration measured by employment over the period 1951–68.[3]

Merger activity has been virtually all-pervasive in the lead and lead alloys trade since 1951. The Lead Industries Group acquired George Johnson (Birmingham) and two of the oldest established smelters (Quirk Barton and St Helens Smelting). During the 1960s the Rio Tinto-Zinc Corporation (RTZ), owners of the Imperial Smelting Corporation, acquired Capper Pass and Son, and 50 per cent of Platt Metals, both of which had some lead production among their output of non-ferrous metals. Firth Cleveland put together a group of four firms after 1961 (British Lead Mills, Brunton, Holman Michell and R. E. Roberts) and there were other mergers among the smaller firms. Only Britannia Lead and H. J. Enthoven and Sons of the larger firms have not expanded externally since 1951. Very tentative calculations suggest that three-firm concentration by gross output increased by 5 percentage points up to 1968.[4]

Evely and Little gave two firms as being most important in cast iron pipes – Allied Ironfounders and Federated Foundries.[5] These firms specialised in rainwater goods, the subsector of the trade which declined after 1951. Pressure pipes increased their share from 1951 to 1963, and the two major firms in that subsector merged in 1960, when Stewarts and Lloyds (with Stanton Ironwork) acquired Staveley Iron and Chemical from the Iron and Steel Holding and Realisation Agency (ISHRA). Stewarts and Lloyds and some other smaller interests were brought into the British Steel Corporation in 1967. Meanwhile, Allied Ironfounders and Federated Foundries merged in 1964 and purchased two small iron-

[1] National Board for Prices and Incomes, *Report No. 133. Portland Cement Prices*, Cmnd 4215, London, HMSO, 1969.

[2] See Hart, Utton and Walshe, *Mergers and Concentration in British Industry*, pp. 77–80, and chapter 4 below.

[3] See Department of Trade and Industry, *Report on the Census of Production 1968*, vol. 23, London, HMSO, 1971; Monopolies Commission, *Report on the Supply of Cigarettes and Tobacco and of Cigarette and Tobacco Machinery*, HC 218, London, HMSO, 1961.

[4] See Annual Reports of the firms mentioned; *Non Ferrous Metal Works of the World*, London, Metal Bulletin (various issues); J. W. F. Rowe, *Price Mechanisms for Lead and Zinc*, New York, International Lead and Zinc Study Group, 1966.

[5] *Concentration in British Industry*, p. 119.

founders in subsequent years, before being themselves acquired by Glyn-wed in 1969. Employment concentration in this trade has undoubtedly increased as a result, probably by more than 10 percentage points for the three leading concerns over the period 1951–69.[1]

The sugar and glucose trade is partially dealt with elsewhere.[2] Manbré and Garton acquired Martineaus in 1959, Westburn Sugar Refineries in 1965 and a small glucose concern, Valentin Ord and Nagle, in the early 1960s.[3] In 1964 Tate and Lyle acquired George Clark and Son, a concern manufacturing brewing sugar, from Brown and Polson. Brown and Polson, itself the subsidiary of Corn Products (subsequently CPC International), a United States firm, took over five firms in glucose, brewing sugars and caramel during the period 1959–64.[4] From the 1968 Census of Production it is possible to establish that three-firm concentration of gross output has advanced by a minimum of 3 percentage points since 1951.

Developments in the trade in cotton thread should of course be viewed in the light of the switch to synthetic threads. New firms have entered the sewing thread market as a whole (for example, Barbour Threads of Northern Ireland and Perivale-Gütermann), while some firms have switched out of cotton altogether (Newroyd, William Paton, Healey Brothers and Highams). However, in cotton thread alone, a trade which Coats Patons and English Sewing still dominated by 1971, there had been virtually no change from the eight-firm employment concentration of 94 per cent in 1951: that is, while small firms have left the trade, the two leading firms have not been slow to diversify their product-mix in response to market pressure.

In summary, a variety of sources suggest that of the eight trades with histories of many-firm amalgamations, seven had further external growth by the leading firms. As for the durability of oligopoly in these trades, there were seven cases of increased concentration and one of no significant change.

Large-firm amalgamations

Mergers appear to have been rather less important in this group of seven trades selected by Evely and Little than in the group considered above.

The Monopolies and Restrictive Practices Commission showed that although the British Match Corporation had only 49 per cent of the voting

---

[1] See *Financial Times*, 10 December 1970, p. 21; International Trade Centre, *The Market for Selected Cast Iron Products in the UK and France*, Geneva, UNCTAD/GATT, 1968; British Steel Corporation Annual Reports and Accounts.

[2] Hart, Utton and Walshe, *Mergers and Concentration in British Industry*, pp. 75–7; 'partially' because glucose (4 per cent of trade sales in 1963) was not covered.

[3] Monopolies Commission, *Report on the Supply of Starch, Glucose and Modified Starches*, HC 615, London, HMSO, 1971, p. 6.

[4] Ibid. paras. 46–8.

power on the boards of two of its main competitors – Maguire (Northern Ireland) and United Match Industries – it nevertheless effectively controlled them.[1] Since that time Maguire has become a *de jure* subsidiary of British Match, while United Match Industries went into liquidation in the late 1960s. British Match is now virtually the only producer of matches in the United Kingdom (a new company, the Consolidated Match Company, appeared in early 1972). The subtrade in firelighters, were it still part of the match trade, would have contributed some 15–20 per cent to 1968 sales compared with roughly 6 per cent in 1951.[2] However, this enlarged contribution from a relatively more fragmented subtrade has not decreased concentration. Two firms – Reckitt and Colman and the Jeyes Group – control upwards of three quarters of the market. This meant that by 1968 three firms contributed over 93 per cent of sales, whereas in 1951 six-firm concentration by gross output was 93 per cent.

In transmission chains, Renold acquired the Perry Chain Company, the only other leading company mentioned by Evely and Little, in the late 1950s. However, three other companies – Borg-Warner, Ewart Chainbelt and Metal Pressings (the last is a small manufacturer of bicycle chains) – still remain to claim about one third or less of the trade. That is, instead of five companies sharing the trade as in 1951, in 1971 there were only four (and it is doubtful whether Metal Pressings had sufficient employees to be classed as a large firm by the Census).

Both ICI and Explosives and Chemical Products, the only non-government firms at present producing explosives for sale in the United Kingdom, have grown by acquisition since 1951.[3] ICI's acquisitions include the Colliery Explosives Company and Burrowite Explosives, while the Thames Nitrogen Company was acquired by Explosives and Chemical Products during the 1960s. ICI became the sole maker of detonators when Yorkshire Electric Detonator left the business in early 1972, and it also enjoys a virtual monopoly in ammunition (although a trivial share of the trade in sporting cartridges is still 'independent'). Nevertheless, concentration has remained virtually unchanged in this trade since 1951, because the fireworks subtrade, with six or seven manufacturers still producing, has almost doubled its proportionate sales (from 6·9 to 12·2 per cent over the period 1951–68).

ICI sold its rights in the trade in incandescent mantles to Falks Veritas in 1945. Falks Veritas acquired one or two other brand rights in the 1940s and 1950s. By 1972, Falks Veritas was the sole British producer of gas

---

[1] *Report on the Supply and Export of Matches and the Supply of Matchmaking Machinery*, HC 161, London, HMSO, 1953.

[2] The 1968 Census separated firelighters from matches. Both matches and firelighters were in volume 125 of the 1963 Census under miscellaneous manufacturing industries, but matches are in volume 39 of the 1968 Census under explosives, matches and fireworks.

[3] S. Fordham, *High Explosives and Propellants*, London, Pergamon, 1966.

mantles and, clearly, concentration has increased in this declining trade.[1]

Zinc is one of the few trades where sales concentration has decreased. The share of smelters' zinc and zinc alloys in the trade has declined relatively to the share of zinc alloy pressure die castings. Along with this change, the Imperial Smelting Corporation, an RTZ subsidiary, saw its share of sales decline from 60–5 per cent in 1951 to 40–5 per cent in 1963.[2] Whereas the share of gross output of the top five firms was 86 per cent in 1951, their share of sales in 1963 was 69 per cent. Perhaps in response to this trend, RTZ acquired in 1968 a 30 per cent interest in London Zinc Mills and a 50 per cent interest in Platt Metals, a general non-ferrous metals firm. In 1970, it also acquired Pillar, which had some zinc die castings capacity. But these purchases (and the acquisition of W. E. Martin, a zinc sheet producer, by Enfield Rolling Mills in the late 1950s) did not offset the overall tendency towards declining concentration in the trade.

Similarly, there have been no mergers of importance in the tin trade since 1951. In 1971 two firms dominated the smelter's tin subsector – Consolidated Tin Smelters with a capacity of 35,000–40,000 tons at a plant in Kirkby, and RTZ (through Capper Pass acquired in 1967), which had a plant at North Ferriby with an annual capacity of 15,000 tons. In the solder subsector, Enthoven, Lead Industries (which acquired George Johnson (Birmingham), a tinfoil and sheet producer, in 1967) and RTZ dominate, but have still not extended that domination to register any significant change in concentration since 1951. Informal estimates suggest that concentration of sales or gross output could have either increased or decreased by 2 or 3 percentage points on a three-firm basis. The 1963 Census registered a decline in five-firm sales concentration from 91·2 per cent to 89·3 per cent for the period 1958–63, during which there was a very significant shift in the proportions of sales derived from refined tin and solder; but there was no such pronounced shift between 1951 and 1963.

In 1966, Kraft Foods, the second ranking firm in the 'domestic use' sector of the margarine trade, acquired Mitcham Foods, which produced some catering and domestic margarines. Otherwise the firms in this sector have not been noticeably acquisitive. Unilever has increased its share of the domestic sector over the period 1958–68 by virtue of successful new product launches and the ability of its cheap brand (Echo) to more than hold its

---

[1] See *Financial Times*, 10 December 1971, p. 29. Falks Veritas managed to make a return (pre-tax profits as a proportion of net current assets) of 34·3 per cent for the year ended 30 June 1971 in this virtually extinct trade.

[2] E. J. Cocks and B. Walters, *A History of the Zinc Smelting Industry in Britain*, London, Harrap, 1968, pp. 202–3; and Census of Production 1951, vol. 3G, table 8, and 1963, vol. 40, p. 14.

own against retailers' 'own label' brands.[1] These two factors making for an increase in concentration, together with the relative decline in importance of non-domestic margarine sales since 1951 (which has a larger number of firms supplying it than has the domestic sector), have helped to increase concentration by a few percentage points over the 1951 level. Informal estimates suggest that three firms – Unilever, Kraft and the Co-operative Wholesale Society (CWS) – had, in 1971, a rather larger share in gross output than the four firms sharing 79 per cent of gross output in 1951.[2]

Asbestos cement was classified by Evely and Little as an internalexpansion trade. This product is also covered by the present study in chapter 3 (see pages 38–9). It is argued there that the product should be allocated to the external-expansion group; that Evely and Little were misled by their sources. We now have the definitive account of the development of concentration in this trade.[3] The major event was the merger of the two leading firms in the late 1920s; the combine then went on to acquire two minor works. During the period 1958–63 the internal growth of small firms contributed to the decline in five-firm sales concentration from 98·3 to 94·2 per cent. However, over the two decades from 1951 to 1971 four-firm concentration by gross output changed barely at all, being 92 per cent at both dates.[4] There were no mergers of capacity in the trade after the war.

In summary, for the group of trades with histories of large-firm amalgamations, mergers have played a rather less important role in changing industrial structure since 1951 than among the group where many firms amalgamated. Nevertheless, all but one of the trades with large-firm amalgamations have seen at least one merger since 1951. There were four cases of increase in concentration, one case of a decrease and three cases of no significant change.

External growth by piecemeal acquisition

After 1951 mergers were experienced in five of the nine trades in this group – spirit rectifying, fertilisers, iron and steel tubes, tinplate, and floorcoverings.

The case of the spirit distilling trade is partially described elsewhere.[5]

---

[1] R. Harris and A. Seldon, *Advertising in Action*, London, Hutchinson, 1962, pp. 271–4; J. H. van Stuyvenberg (ed.), *Margarine: an economic, social and scientific history, 1869–1969*, Liverpool University Press, 1969; National Board for Prices and Incomes, *Report No. 147. Margarine and Compound Cooking Fats*, Cmnd 4368, London, HMSO, 1970; *Financial Times*, 11 February 1972.

[2] It can also be noted that the five-firm sales concentration in margarine increased from 88·1 per cent in 1958 to 92·8 per cent in 1963 (Census of Production 1963, vol. 131, table 5).

[3] Monopolies Commission *Report on Asbestos and Certain Asbestos Products*, HC 3, London, HMSO, 1973.   [4] Ibid. p. 27.

[5] See the study of developments in blended whisky in Hart, Utton and Walshe, *Mergers and Concentration in British Industry*, pp. 85–7; also chapter 3 below.

No mergers occurred in this field which could have increased concentration; indeed there was some tendency for concentration to decline as the brewers extended their distilling interests.[1] However, even by 1968 the brewers had not entrenched themselves sufficiently to offset the concentration increase which occurred over the period 1951–8 (five-firm concentration of 85 per cent by gross output in 1951 had grown to 96·1 per cent by sales in 1958). In 1968 three firms (Distillers, Teacher and Bells) had 85 per cent or more of the home market,[2] while Distillers, International Distillers and Vintners (IDV) and Highland Distilleries dominated United Kingdom whisky exports.

IDV was the purchaser in the only notable merger of the spirit rectifying trade after 1951: in 1962 it acquired Gilbeys and their gin interests were thus added to the two thirds of the vodka market claimed by IDV.[3] Distillers, James Burrough and IDV probably accounted for over 92 per cent of gross output by the sector by 1970 – an increase on the level obtaining in 1951 of over 5 percentage points.

In weighing machines, Averys and George Salter, the two dominant firms, do not appear to have made any acquisitions since 1951. Internal growth apparently increased concentration by gross output above the 1951 level of 80 per cent for the top six firms.[4] Almost certainly the two linked major firms had more than four fifths of production between them in 1971.

The position is more ambiguous in soap and glycerine, where Unilever and Procter and Gamble dominate production of soap flakes and powder.[5] Information regarding the other, rather less concentrated, subsectors of this trade (toilet soap, glycerine, fatty acids, soap base, hard soap, scourers, shaving soap and shampoos) is difficult to assemble. One source yields a rough estimate of three-firm concentration by sales of 80–5 per cent in 1954,[6] distinctly higher than 75 per cent, the three-firm concentration by gross output in 1951, and this impression is confirmed by the Prices and Incomes Board.[7] However, it may be noted that in soap alone five-firm

[1] Five-firm sales concentration declined from 96·1 per cent in 1958 to 94·2 per cent in 1963.

[2] Economist Intelligence Unit, *Retail Business*, no. 123, May 1968.

[3] See below, chapter 4, for an account of concentration in gin production.

[4] Cf. a stockbrokers' report, 'The engineering industry, book II', Panmure, Gordon and Co., 1969, p. 87: 'The possibility of Averys obtaining a larger share of the existing market for weighing and testing machinery can be ruled out; the group already almost completely dominates this area, and at the same time owns 15·4 per cent of the equity of George Salter'.

[5] They had a joint share of some 97 per cent in British production in 1964, see Monopolies Commission, *Household Detergents, Report on the supply of household detergents*, HC 105, London, HMSO, 1966.

[6] H. R. Edwards, *Competition and Monopoly in the British Soap Industry*, Oxford, Clarendon Press, 1962, pp. 239–41.

[7] National Board for Prices and Incomes, *Report No. 4. Prices of Household and Toilet Soaps, Soap Powders and Soap Flakes, and Soapless Detergents*, Cmnd 2791, London, HMSO, 1965, pp. 2–3.

sales concentration fell from 83·2 per cent in 1958 to 80·9 per cent in 1963.[1] The finding of an increase in concentration up to 1966 should be treated with caution. No mergers appear to have taken place in the trade since 1951.

Both the major firms in the fertiliser trade, ICI and Fisons, acquired smaller concerns after 1951. ICI bought a fertiliser plant from the Scottish CWS in 1956, while Richardsons Chemical Manure and the Ulster Manure Company were purchased in the later 1950s, and in 1966 a 50 per cent interest was acquired in Hargreaves Fertilisers. Fisons' purchases came during the period 1964–6, when it acquired brand rights from British Basic Slag, and gained control of West Norfolk Fertilisers as well as International Toxin Products.[2] The entry of Shell into fertilisers, first with imports and, during the 1960s, with domestically produced output, did not offset the tendency towards increased concentration in the trade. Indeed, as might be expected, Shell's scale was large (in 1971 it produced roughly 9 per cent of British output) and together the three leading firms produced some 79 per cent of British output in 1971 compared with three-firm concentration by gross output of 73 per cent in 1951.[3]

Tube Investments and Stewarts and Lloyds, the two leading firms in steel tubes, also continued to concentrate the trade by piecemeal acquisition after 1951. Stewarts and Lloyds acquired the Extended Surface Tube Company in the early 1960s, while Tube Investments acquired Fulton (TI), British Steel Golf Shafts, Markland Scowcroft, Associated Tube Companies (Compoflex) and United Flexible Metallic Tubing, during the period 1963–9. In 1967 Stewarts and Lloyds became part of the British Steel Corporation, which went on to acquire the Wellington Tube Works in 1970. From the Annual Reports and Accounts of the leading concerns, it is possible to establish that two firms shared roughly 85 per cent of sales in 1968 as against four-firm concentration by gross output of 84 per cent in 1951.

The history of merger and atrophy in the tinplate trade is summarised in chapter 4. Steel nationalisation in 1967 brought virtually 100 per cent of production into one firm, whereas the three-firm concentration by gross output was 74 per cent in 1951.

There were no further notable mergers of capacity in the motorcycle trade after 1951, although in 1966 Manganese Bronze combined its

---

[1] Census of Production 1963, part 131, table 5.

[2] Mennel, *Takeover*, pp. 67–8, notes three other acquisitions by the two major firms during the 1950s – in 1954 ICI acquired Plant Protection and Fisons purchased Pest Control, while in 1960 Fisons acquired Pickering and West.

[3] See Monopolies Commission, *Report on the Supply of Chemical Fertilisers*, HC 267, London, HMSO, 1959; National Board for Prices and Incomes, *Report No. 28. Prices of Compound Fertilizers*, Cmnd 3228, London, HMSO, 1967; and *Financial Times*, 20 February 1973, p. 1.

Norton Villiers engine concern vertically with Associated Motor Cycles. Whereas four-firm concentration by gross output was 82 per cent in 1951, it has been observed that, in the late 1960s: '... four firms, two large and two small ... accounted for over 90 per cent of the motorcycle industry's volume of output'.[1] Three-wheeled vehicles, which increased their share of trade sales from 3·8 per cent in 1951 to 22·6 per cent in 1970,[2] are virtually all made by one company, Reliant Motor. Thus, three firms controlled roughly 93 per cent of trade sales in 1970.

The final trade in this group, floorcoverings, has suffered competition from newer thermoplastic products and carpets since 1951. In a declining market, the leading firm, Nairn, responded by acquiring Jas. Williamson and Son in 1962 and North British Linoleum in 1964. Later, in 1966–7, British Steel Constructions, without a previous interest in the trade, acquired Tayside Floorcloth and Barry Staines. Nairn-Williamson, Thomas Witter and Dundee Linoleum controlled about 88 per cent of the trade between them by the end of the 1960s, and Dundee phased itself out of linoleum production in 1970. This left three firms controlling over 95 per cent of production, compared to three with 72 per cent of gross output in 1951.

In summary, there was significant merger activity in five out of the nine trades in this group. On the question of the persistence of oligopoly, all nine appear to have increased in concentration after 1951, although soap and glycerine is a possible exception.

HIGH-CONCENTRATION TRADES WITH INTERNALLY EXPANDED LEADING FIRMS

Positions of market dominance can be achieved by internally expanding leading firms from an initial situation where there are many firms, or it may be that the trade has always had few firms and that this explains high concentration. Evely and Little's allocation of trades to these two categories was that razors and ice cream were in the first, whereas rubber tyres, man-made fibres and mineral oil refining were in the second.

---

[1] R. A. Cooper and K. Hartley, *Export Performance and the Pressure of Demand: a study of firms*, London, Allen and Unwin, 1970, p. 164. See also Moodies Industries and Commodities Service, *Basic Review of Cycles*, 18 January 1971, which gives Birmingham Small Arms 80 per cent of 'the total output' and Norton Villiers 'a 12 per cent market share'; 'The management skid in the two wheeler business', *Business*, vol. 95, May 1965, pp. 22–32; and *Financial Times*, 13 June 1972, p. 14, which notes that Royal Enfield and Velocette went out of the business in 1970–1. Manganese Bronze now owns Royal Enfield's patents.

[2] Department of Trade and Industry, *Business Monitor: production series*, no. P2, March 1971.

Many-firm trades

In both razors and ice cream the leadership of the major firms was threatened after 1951. In razors, the response of Gillette Industries to the intrusion of Wilkinson Sword (with various innovations around the theme of stainless steel blades and their polymer coating) has been simply to surrender market leadership and hope to regain it with their own innovations (for example, polytetrofluoroethylene coatings, band cartridge razors and platinum–chrome alloy coatings). By 1972 Gillette had 35 to 40 per cent of sales and Wilkinson some 50 to 55 per cent, and four-firm concentration by gross output, which was 98 per cent in 1951, had not changed by more than 1 or 2 percentage points either way.[1]

The response of Unilever and Lyons to the advent of new competition in the ice cream trade during the 1950s and 1960s was to acquire many of the competing businesses and, as a consequence, the two major firms controlled over 80 per cent of large-firm output in 1970, whereas in 1951 three-firm concentration by gross output was 77 per cent.[2]

Few-firm trades

In rubber tyres and tubes, Dunlop has acquired a number of firms very much smaller than itself in an effort to retain its leadership,[3] but this activity has not prevented concentration declining up to 1970 by 1 or 2 points from the three-firm ratio by gross output of 76 per cent in 1951.

The Monopolies Commission has reported the fates of most of the smaller firms in the rayon trade.[4] Courtaulds acquired British Celanese, Harbens, British Enkalon, James Nelson and Kirklees over the seven-year period 1957–63, while Chemstrand (now Monsanto Textiles) took over Lansil in 1962. Other firms left the industry during the 1950s (British Bemberg and North British Rayon). Although Monsanto and British Enkalon have developed their own nylon capacity since British Nylon Spinners (the joint Courtaulds–ICI concern) held its monopoly, Courtaulds and ICI still dominate production in both rayon and nylon. In 1970, Courtaulds, ICI and Monsanto had about 97 per cent of man-made fibre capacity between them, as against a three-firm concentration by gross output of 81 per cent in 1951.[5]

---

[1] See *Financial Times*, 15 January 1965; Economist Intelligence Unit, *Retail Business*, no. 155, January 1971.

[2] See chapter 3 below for a study of ice cream.

[3] See chapter 3 below for a short appreciation of post-1951 developments.

[4] Monopolies Commission, *Report on Man-made Cellulosic Fibres*, HC 130, London, HMSO, 1968, especially app. 7.

[5] See, for example, a stockbrokers' report, 'Renaissance in textiles', Strauss Turnbull, 1967, for one of the many accounts of capacity given in non-official sources. Figures in C. F. Pratten, *Economies of Scale in Manufacturing Industry*, Cambridge University Press, 1971, pp. 60–1, confirm the picture given by Strauss Turnbull.

New entry was responsible for a decline in concentration in mineral oil refining. The capacity of the top three firms in the trade was just over 77 per cent in 1968,[1] as against a gross output ratio of 93 per cent by three firms in 1951. The only merger activity in the trade concerned two small specialist refiners (Lobitos Oilfields and Manchester Oil Refinery, now both part of Burmah Oil), who combined in 1960 and contributed under 1 per cent of British capacity in 1965. Much more important were the entry of Mobil (1953), Regent – now Texaco (early 1960s) and Gulf Oil (Great Britain) (mid-1960s), which diluted the dominance of Esso, Shell and British Petroleum.

In summary, four of the five internal-growth trades experienced mergers after 1951, a break with their previous history. However, the consequences for the persistence of tight oligopoly are ambiguous. There were two cases of increases, two of decreases and one of no change in the level of concentration over the period from 1951 up to recent years.

HIGH-CONCENTRATION TRADES WHERE LEADING FIRMS HAVE EXPANDED IN DIFFERENT WAYS

In this section the task will be to classify these trades as dependent on either external or internal growth, wherever it is clear that one kind of growth path has been dominant. Evely and Little classified six trades as 'differing' – starch, photographic plates and films, bicycles, seed crushing and oil refining, cinematograph film printing, and valves and cathode ray tubes.

Many-firm trades

The Monopolies Commission shows that the starch trade has expanded externally.[2] This applied to both Brown and Polson, and Reckitt and Colman, who were the two leading firms in 1951. Brown and Polson acquired William McKean and William Wotherspoon in 1922, and was itself acquired in 1935 by Corn Products Refining, which in turn had acquired Nicholls Nagel in 1923. The enlarged firm went on to acquire Farina Dextrin in 1948 and Dextrines in 1959. Evely and Little describe the external growth of Reckitt and Colman.[3] New entry since 1951, notably by Tunnel Refineries and Manbré and Garton, could have been expected to decrease concentration, but there seems to be little evidence for this. The assumption here, in the absence of direct evidence to the contrary, is that no great change has occurred since 1951 in three-firm concentration by

---

[1] See, for example, *Chemical Industry Handbook, 1969*, chap. VI.

[2] Monopolies Commission, *Report on the Supply of Starch*; also J. W. Knight, *The Starch Industry*, London, Pergamon, 1969.

[3] *Concentration in British Industry*, p. 127.

gross output of 82 per cent. The Monopolies Commission, reporting in 1971, should have allowed us to derive a recent estimate. However, the Commission was interested primarily in the supply situation, so that they reported simply shares of the market, including imports sold by the leading firms without further processing. One series of plausible assumptions about the leaders' shares of unprocessed imports yields a three-firm concentration level by sales of 88 per cent.[1]

The trade in photographic plates and films encompasses photographic film and paper, sensitised document copying papers and other sensitised papers. The entry of new firms into sensitised paper production would have decreased concentration below the four-firm level by gross output of 90 per cent in 1951. However, Ozalid is now the largest firm in the sub-sector and has grown consistently by acquisition. The most important acquisitions in the 1960s were Nig Securities in 1968, E. N. Mason and Sons in 1969 and, more recently, Criterion Plates Papers Films. This policy has left Ozalid with only two substantial competitors – Admel International and GAF (Great Britain), which are both subsidiaries of American corporations – and a few smaller competitors in more specialised papers.[2] Kodak and Ilford share the remainder of the trade – Kodak have about two thirds of British film production.[3] Kodak's lead in this field will be advanced as colour film increases its market share at the expense of black and white, because Kodak contributed over 90 per cent of United Kingdom colour film production.[4] It is probably safest to assume that there has been no change in concentration since 1951.[5] If we had been allocating this trade to a growth category from the standpoint of 1970, the acquisitions of Ozalid and Ilford would have placed the trade in the external-expansion group. But Kodak was the major firm in the trade in 1951 and only Ilford, with a minority share of the trade as a whole, showed a propensity to acquire other firms up to 1951. Thus the trade has to be classified as growing internally.

Evely and Little classed the bicycle trade as 'differing' in the belief that, until 1951, Raleigh Industries had expanded primarily by internal growth.[6] However, another source claimed that Raleigh 'has absorbed

---

[1] Monopolies Commission, *Report on the Supply of Starch*, paras. 13, 17 and 45, and app. 1.

[2] For example, Harper and Tunstall, and A. West and Partners.

[3] Monopolies Commission, *Report on the Supply and Processing of Colour Film*, HC 1, London, HMSO, 1966, para. 79, implies that Ilford, the smaller of the two remaining photographic film firms, has acquired a few small producers of black and white film since 1945. Ilford, after ICI had acquired it in 1967, was sold off to CIBA-Geigy (UK) in 1969.

[4] Ibid. para. 11.

[5] Calculations based on information gleaned from trade sources and the Monopolies Commission suggest that the four leading firms (Kodak, Ozalid, Ilford and GAF) probably contributed about 90–5 per cent of sales in the trade in 1971, but this disregards the contribution of the few small firms producing specialised sensitised papers.

[6] *Concentration in British Industry*, pp. 127–8.

many of its competitors'.[1] For example, Raleigh acquired the Rudge-Whitworth concern in 1943 and the rights to worldwide production of Humber cycles in 1946.[2] It later acquired the Triumph Cycle Company in 1956 and the bicycle interests of the externally expanded Birmingham Small Arms in 1957. Eventually, in 1961, Raleigh merged with the externally expanded Tube Investments, which acquired the important new entrant of the 1960s, Moulton Bicycles, in 1967.[3] Because both of the major firms in 1951 – Raleigh and Birmingham Small Arms – grew to some extent by acquisition, the trade may be classed as expanding externally. In 1951 three-firm concentration by gross output was 68 per cent, whereas one source stated that its sample of three bicycle firms in the late 1960s 'represented over 90 per cent of the industry's output'.[4]

The proper classification for seed crushing and oil refining is difficult to find. Merger activity seems to have been confined to Unilever before 1951.[5] The structure of the seed crushing subsector described by one source appears to give Unilever something less than 50 per cent of the trade,[6] while oil refining is more fragmented than seed crushing. But no reliable decision can be made here, nor can an estimate of the change in concentration since 1951 be attempted, because too large a variety of products is classified in the trade. Although the large number of exits by small firms would argue, *ceteris paribus*, for an increase in concentration, the changing structure of leadership in fish and marine animal oils (see chapter 3 below) may have produced a decrease in trade concentration since 1951.

Few-firm trades

Since 1951, both the internally expanded leading firms in the cinematograph film printing trade have made acquisitions. Technicolor, the largest firm, acquired Henderson Film Laboratories in 1963, and Humphries Film Laboratories acquired Filmatic Laboratories in 1968. Moreover, Technicolor acquired the colour film processing plant of Associated British Picture Corporation in 1968 – a deal which gave the latter 30 per cent of Technicolor's equity. However, neither Technicolor nor Humphries grew externally before 1951, and their joint share of the trade has always been far larger than that of Rank, the externally expanded firm.

---

[1] *The Cycle Industry*, London, Political and Economic Planning, 1949, p. 112.

[2] See N. B. Hudson, 'The growth and structure of the bicycle industry' (unpublished) 1960, pp. 174ff.

[3] M. C. Wyatt, 'The bicycle industry', *Westminster Bank Review*, May 1966, pp. 42–51.

[4] Cooper and Hartley, *Export Performance*, pp. 191–2.

[5] See *Annual Congress, Report of Proceedings*, London, International Association of Seed Crushers, 1960, pp. 95–6; also C. Wilson, *Unilever 1945–1965*, London, Cassell, 1968, pp. 163–5.

[6] International Trade Centre, *The Market for Oilcake in Western Europe* and *The Market for Cottonseed Oil in Five European Countries and Japan*, Geneva, UNCTAD/GATT 1966 and 1967 respectively.

Until 1951, Rank was the only firm in the trade to grow externally and did not at any time have more than a fifth of trade employment. Thus we may classify the trade on the whole as one of internal growth. Concentration on a three-firm employment basis appears to have increased from 61 per cent in 1951 to over 70 per cent by 1969.[1]

Because in 1951 Philips (the internal-growth firm) controlled less than 50 per cent of the trade in valves and cathode ray tubes, and because most of the other members of the trade grew externally, we may classify the trade as growing externally.[2] Moreover, Philips' growth up to 1951 was not all internal; Mullard was acquired in 1927 and E. K. Cole sold its valve interests to Mullard in 1938. Philips went on to acquire the British Tungsram Radio Works in 1952, and Pye with the Cathodeon valve subsidiary in 1967. The valve interests of the General Electric Company (GEC), which had acquired the remaining 50 per cent of the M-O Valve Company it did not already own from Electric and Musical Industries in 1956, were joined by those of English Electric when the two merged in 1968. The valve interests of Associated Electric Industries (AEI) were sold by GEC to Thorn Electric in 1969 and, by 1969, Thorn had also acquired 51 per cent of RCA Colour Tubes, the only significant new entrant after 1951. Thus the three-firm concentration by sales of 83 per cent as indicated by the Monopolies Commission (one point higher than the three-firm concentration by gross output in 1951) will have been affected by the addition of British Tungsram and Cathodeon to Philips, by the merging of GEC and English Electric, and by the rather more important addition of Thorn and its RCA Colour Tubes interests to the AEI capacity. That is, concentration has almost certainly increased since 1951, especially in view of the greater importance of cathode ray tubes, where Thorn and Mullard have a virtual duopoly. Trade sources indicate that cathode ray tubes constituted over three quarters of sales in 1970.

In summary, we may classify three of these six cases as expanding externally, two as expanding internally, while one must remain an unresolved difficulty. In five of the six trades there was evidence of merger activity after 1951; three have increased concentration since 1951, two did not change and for the remaining trade no estimate could be attempted.

[1] See National Board for Prices and Incomes, *Report No. 131. Pay of Certain Employees in the Film Processing Industry*, Cmnd 4185, London, HMSO, 1969, paras. 7 and 25; trade directories; Evely and Little, *Concentration in British Industry*, pp. 240–3.

[2] Monopolies and Restrictive Practices Commission, *Report on the Supply of Electronic Valves and Cathode Ray Tubes*, HC 16, London, HMSO, 1957.

SUMMARY OF FINDINGS

Our findings may be summarised under five heads. Of the thirty-six trades in Evely and Little's sample, twenty-eight may be classified as growing externally and seven as growing internally before 1951 (one trade – seed crushing and oil refining – could not be classified). For the period since 1951 there is some evidence of mergers in twenty-eight of the thirty-six trades; only in eight trades was there no traceable merger activity.

Of the seven trades classified as expanding internally up to 1951, six have seen acquisitions by the leading firms since that date, but in two cases (mineral oil refining and cinematograph film printing) these acquisitions made a very minor contribution to total growth of market share. As a consequence, we may conclude that, after 1951, large firms in four of the seven internal-expansion trades changed their original method of increasing their market shares.

In twenty-two of the twenty-eight trades classified as expanding externally, there was some evidence of further merger activity after 1951. The final result depends on unofficial estimates of concentration which, in some cases, must be treated with caution. Of the thirty-five trades for which some estimate could be made, twenty-five experienced an increase in concentration after 1951, three experienced a decrease in concentration, and in the remaining seven no significant change in concentration could be detected.

It thus appears that, on the whole, monopoly or tight oligopoly has tended to persist in this selection of trades, though this result must be interpreted carefully, if only because all increases in concentration are not equally significant. For example, in wallpaper a slight increase in concentration was attended by a significant alteration in the competitive structure of the industry (quite apart from the competition of new products), because a near monopoly was transformed into a duopoly in the course of the two decades after 1951. Again, in razors, where no significant change in concentration was registered, we saw a classic example of the 'sleeping giant' having market leadership wrested from it and a monopoly was transformed into a duopoly. On the other hand, there are instances where very minor increases in concentration have been the outward sign of highly significant 'tightening' in the market structure towards monopoly or near-monopoly. In industries where concentration ratios were above 80 or 90 per cent in 1951, very dramatic increases could not be expected. Nevertheless, a reduction since then in the number of major competing firms represents a significant change in the degree of competition, even if the concentration ratio is unaltered. Some trades where this applies are cast iron pipes, salt, explosives and fireworks, and incandescent mantles.

CHAPTER 3

MERGERS IN PRODUCTS WITH MONOPOLY OR NEAR-MONOPOLY MARKETS IN 1958

INTRODUCTION

In this and the following chapter the business history of thirty-two mono-poly or near-monopoly products will be traced in order to see what role, if any, mergers have played in producing high degrees of concentration. The present chapter surveys all products for which the 1963 Census of Production gave a five-firm concentration ratio by sales of 90 per cent or more in 1958; there were twenty-four products in this category out of a total of 277 products distinguished. The next chapter surveys additional products for which concentration ratios were not given in the 1963 Census because of the official prohibition on possible disclosure of informa-tion relating to individual firms; concentration in these eight products was certainly above 90 per cent.

The twenty-four products are listed in tables 3.1 and 3.2. Table 3.1 gives eight products where mergers played a major role in achieving the degree of monopolisation recorded by 1958, while table 3.2 gives the products where internal expansion was mainly responsible for monopolisation. Perhaps the most notable feature of these tables is that no less than eight of the twenty-four products (one third) are in the processed food and drink industry, while most other industrial orders are under-represented. Indeed, textiles, clothing and footwear are not represented at all. Because of deficiencies in the basic statistical source some famous monopolies are missing, such as man-made fibres, matches, explosives and tinplate, to name a few. However, some of these trades are covered in chapter 4, while others have been discussed by Evely and Little, so that, as we shall see in chapter 5, our conclusions are ultimately based on an adequately representative sample.

Thirteen of the products experienced an increase in concentration over the period 1958–63, and eleven a decrease. It must be made clear at once, however, that we are not solely interested in the short period between 1958 and 1963. Our canvas is a large one and the period 1958–63 is considered here primarily as a point of reference. Where reasons for the change in concentration between 1958 and 1963 are established which seem interesting in their own right, they are outlined in the text.

If the reader has doubts about the criterion of a 90 per cent five-firm sales concentration to indicate monopolised or tightly oligopolised markets, he is not alone in this. However, as explained in chapter 1, we

Table 3.1. *External-expansion products with 90 per cent concentration or more in 1958*

Percentages

MLH		Sales concentration ratios[a]	
		1958	1963
311 (part)	Steel sheet	91·1	94·2
322 (part)	Tin and tin alloys	91·2	89·3
483(1)	Wallpaper	91·6	95·1
239(1) (part)	Blended whisky	96·1	94·2
271(1)	Dyestuffs	97·1	93·7
463 (part)	Safety glass	97·7	96·6
469(2) (part)	Asbestos cement goods	98·3	94·2
364 (part)	Gramophone records	99·0	97·4

SOURCE: Census of Production 1963, part 131, table 5.
[a] Based on top 5 firms.

Table 3.2. *Internal-expansion products with 90 per cent concentration or more in 1958*

Percentages

MLH		Sales concentration ratio[a]	
		1958	1963
336 (part)	Crawler tractors	90·1	98·0
275(2) (part)	Detergents	90·4	84·5
381 (part)	Cars	90·4	91·5
363 (part)	Telegraph and telephone installations	90·4	94·0
215(1) (part)	Condensed and evaporated milk	90·9	93·4
218(2) (part)	Soups	91·1	92·5
271(3) (part)	Synthetic rubber	91·7	99·4
214(1) (part)	Frozen fish	93·2	91·7
491(1)	Rubber tyres and tubes	93·2	94·5
363 (part)	Line apparatus	93·9	96·2
215(2)	Ice cream	94·2	94·6
349(1)	Ball and roller bearings	94·4	85·2
275(1) (part)	Fish and marine animal oils	94·9	92·8
381 (part)	Wheeled tractors	95·4	97·6
229(2) (part)	Coffee extracts and essences	97·9	98·4
218(2) (part)	Frozen vegetables	98·6	93·3

SOURCE: as table 3.1.
[a] Based on top 5 firms.

are limited to the official data, and for the moment the discussion will proceed as if this indicator accurately selects monopoly or tight oligopoly markets. Evely and Little chose a criterion of 67 per cent for high-concentration trades where the number of firms on which the concentration ratio was based was usually three.[1] For comparability with Evely and Little, using the product classification of the 1963 Census which is finer than their trade classification, a higher percentage criterion must be chosen. As Evely and Little argued: 'In general, the more broadly an industry is defined (that is the greater the number and range of the principal products that comprise it) the higher will be the number of business units included and the lower will be its concentration ratio. Thus, concentration ratios for individual products are frequently higher than the concentration ratio for the trade of which they form part.'[2] In the event, a 90 per cent boundary yields enough cases to draw worthwhile conclusions about the role of mergers in monopoly, near-monopoly and tight oligopoly products. A general discussion of how useful the indicator appears to be is postponed until chapter 6.

EXTERNAL-EXPANSION PRODUCTS

The following eight products (see table 3.1) reached their high levels of concentration primarily as the result of mergers.

Blended whisky

The Distillers Company was a merger-intensive firm from 1877, when it was formed by the amalgamation of six grain distilling concerns, until 1925, when a merger with its chief rivals was effected and it produced about 80 per cent of grain and malt whisky output.[3] Distillers' purchases have been characterised as defensive throughout,[4] and acquisition was often followed by closure of the acquired plant. The Chairman explained in 1927 that, including the original six distilleries, the company had acquired twenty-four patent-still distilleries of which only ten were still active; in addition, forty-seven pot-still distilleries had been acquired, and only twenty-seven of these had been operated during the previous season[5].

The other members of the 1925 merger were Buchanan-Dewar and John Walker and Sons. Both Buchanan and Dewar had expanded in the 1890s by acquiring or building malt distilleries, while Walker acquired the Cardow distillery in 1893. Buchanan and Dewar merged in 1915, and in the same year Distillers and Walker jointly acquired the Coleburn-Glenlivet

---

[1] *Concentration in British Industry*, pp. 50–3, where thirty of the trades had three-firm ratios, ten had four-firm ratios, and another ten used five to eight firms.

[2] Ibid. pp. 50–1.   [3] Ibid. p. 121.

[4] R. Wilson, *Scotch, the Formative Years*, London, Constable, 1970, chaps. 28–31.

[5] Ibid. p. 415.

Highland distillery. Numerous small distilleries sold out to the large concerns during the 1914–18 war because of financial difficulties and in 1919 the three members of the 1925 merger, plus John Haig, were considered the leading firms in the trade.[1] Distillers and Haig merged in that year, and the top three companies continued to acquire ailing companies which were unable to ride out the prolonged period of postwar overproduction. Notable purchases occurred in 1922 when Distillers acquired the Distillers Finance Company, which owned many distilleries in Ireland and Scotland, and in 1923 when James Watson was purchased jointly by Buchanan-Dewar and Walker.

The more important purchases after the 1925 merger were Distillers' acquisitions in 1927 of White Horse Distillers, and of the shares not already held in Scottish Malt Distillers, which had been steadily acquiring firms since its formation (from five distilleries) in 1914. In 1937 Distillers acquired Booths Distilleries, mainly a gin concern which also had a few whisky distilleries.[2]

Of the remaining large firms still extant in the post-1945 period, Arthur Bell acquired three distilleries during the interwar period, Teacher acquired one company, while Seager Evans and Hiram Walker and Sons (Scotland) also purchased a number of distillers and blenders.[3] In more recent years, the market pre-eminence of Distillers has dwindled rather, because of both the growth of these latter concerns and the expansion of sales from brewer-owned distilleries.[4]

In summary, high concentration of this product has resulted from piecemeal acquisitions by leading firms and the one tripartite merger of 1925.

Dyestuffs

High concentration in this product (MLH 271) was actively promoted by the government. At the beginning of this century the trade was small and technically backward. Only two producers of any size existed – Levinstein and British Alizarine – while on the eve of the first world war about 90 per cent by weight of British consumption was imported.[5] Before the first world war, two European manufacturers – Farbwercke Hoechst and Badische-Bayer – established plants in the United Kingdom to secure their British patents. Two other firms were important in intermediates for dyestuffs – Read Holliday and Clayton Aniline.[6] There

---

[1] Ibid. p. 411.　　　　　　　　　　[2] See p. 68 below.

[3] On Hiram Walker, see *Investors Chronicle*, 13 November 1937, p. 1112.

[4] See Hart, Utton and Walshe, *Mergers and Concentration in British Industry*, pp. 85–7.

[5] See L. F. Haber, *The Chemical Industry 1900–1930: international growth and technological change*, Oxford, Clarendon Press, 1971; *Report on the Chemical Industry, 1949*, London, Association of British Chemical Manufacturers, 1949; D. W. F. Hardie and J. Davidson-Pratt, *A History of the Modern British Chemical Industry*, London, Pergamon, 1966, pp. 156ff. and part B.

[6] The latter has been controlled by the Swiss firm CIBA since 1911.

were in addition half a dozen or so very small British-owned dyestuff firms.

During the first world war German imports ceased and the need for domestic supplies became urgent. The government promoted production of intermediates (also required for explosives) first by Read Holliday and Clayton Aniline, and later, in 1915, with the formation of British Dyestuffs from the Read Holliday embryo. Production at Levinstein also expanded until, by 1917–18, these two concerns produced about three quarters of British consumption.[1] Levinstein expanded by acquisition during the war: it acquired the Hoechst indigo plant inexpensively from the Custodian of Enemy Property in 1916 and in the same year it purchased the Manchester firm of Claus and Company.[2] Two new entrants to the trade started during the war – L. B. Holliday, making picric acid and dyestuffs, and Solway Dyes (renamed Scottish Dyes in 1919), who were inventors and developers of soluble vat dyes.

Again, in 1918 the government promoted the merger between British Dyestuffs and Levinstein to form the British Dyestuffs Corporation. Using the argument that this was a 'key' industry, the government also introduced protection by issuing licences to import only those dyes not produced domestically.[3] Excess world capacity in dyestuffs and British Dyestuffs' desire to remain the United Kingdom leader probably explain their purchase in 1926 of Scottish Dyes, whose scientists had discovered a number of popular colours. The combine was subsumed in ICI later in the same year and ICI went on to acquire the smaller concern of Oliver and Wilkins in 1928, the medium-sized British Alizarine in 1931 (itself a combination of dyers formed in 1892 to purchase Burt Boulton and Haywood, the owner of an alizarin production process) and Leech Neal in 1936. After the 1926 merger, British Dyestuffs produced some 45–50 per cent of British output, Clayton Aniline 20–5 per cent, L. B. Holliday and British Alizarine together about 15 per cent; the rest of the industry therefore shared 10–20 per cent of output. Thus the joint share of British Dyestuffs and Levinstein had fallen by 1926 and tended to decline thereafter. ICI's share of output – 55–60 per cent during the 1930s – may now be less than 50 per cent.[4]

[1] Haber, *The Chemical Industry*, p. 192. See also p. 190, where it is stated that Levinstein had a dye capacity in 1914 of 5000 tons per annum, which was significantly under-used because British production was only 4000 tons.

[2] Successors to Claus and Ree which had acquired Brook, Simpson and Spiller before 1916, which in turn had acquired Perkin and Sons, one of the first British dyestuff concerns to be established, in 1874.

[3] For details see Haber, *The Chemical Industry*, pp. 140–5.

[4] Cf. National Board for Prices and Incomes, *Report No. 100. Synthetic Organic Dyestuffs and Organic Pigment Prices*, Cmnd 3895, London, HMSO, 1969, para. 13; and W. B. Reddaway, 'The chemical industry' in D. Burn (ed.), *The Structure of British Industry*, vol. I, Cambridge University Press, 1958, pp. 248–9.

The other large firms in the industry have grown internally for the most part. This is true of the Clayton Aniline Company, which in 1966 was responsible for just under one fifth of British output with 1130 employees,[1] and of L. B. Holliday, with 1000 employees mainly in dyestuffs.[2] The Prices and Incomes Board[3] claimed that the only other important British producers were Yorkshire Dyeware and Chemical Company (800 employees in 1966)[4] and Williams (Hounslow) (450 employees in 1966, but less diversified). There were ten other producers in the trade in 1958 and 1963, none of them very large in view of the sales concentration ratio, which declined from 97·1 per cent in 1958 to 93·7 per cent in 1963.

Smaller firms are able to survive by specialising in the production of a few dyes.[5] The production processes are mainly of the batch type, as Hardie and Davidson-Pratt note,[6] so that the plant scale-economies are unimportant. Firm scale-economies are, however, claimed to be important for the development of new products requiring heavy research costs.[7] In fact Scottish Dyes, the successor to a small firm started in the first world war, discovered many of the new dyes of the early 1920s. Under these circumstances it is not possible to explain high concentration as the inevitable result of economies of scale in research. Mergers were first promoted to achieve certain nationally important objectives, then sought by British Dyestuffs and ICI to bolster technical expertise within the company. Since then the smaller firms have been unable to make more than very minor inroads into the shares of the larger, research-intensive firms.

Steel sheet

The full description of this census sector (MLH 311) is 'steel plates and sheets, uncoated, under 3 millimetres thick', but it is normally known simply as 'sheet', which will be the shorthand used here. There is a close similarity between the emergence of high concentration in this product and in tinplate (discussed below, see pages 69–71).

The largest firms in steel sheet in the mid-1920s were John Summers and Sons, Baldwins, John Lysaght and Richard Thomas.[8] Summers acquired Wolverhampton Corrugated Iron during the 1914–18 war and the integrated works of Shelton Iron Steel and Coal in 1920. In 1901 E. P. and W. Baldwin merged with Knight and Crowther and the Blackwall

---

[1] See NBPI, *Synthetic Organic Dyestuffs*, para. 14 and Hardie and Davidson-Pratt, *A History*, p. 284.　　　　[2] Ibid. p. 298.

[3] NBPI, *Synthetic Organic Dyestuffs*, para. 15.

[4] See Hardie and Davidson-Pratt, *A History*, p. 328; the concern was an amalgamation in 1900 of several old concerns supplying dyes to industry.

[5] Like Bottomley and Emerson, James Robinson and Son, Golden Valley Colours, and Hickson and Welch (Holdings).　　　　[6] Ibid. p. 158.

[7] Ibid. p. 159 and NPBI, *Synthetic Organic Dyestuffs*, paras. 27–8.

[8] K. Warren, *The British Iron and Steel Sheet Industry since 1840. An economic geography*, London, G. Bell and Sons, 1970, pp. 106ff.

Galvanised Iron Company. The following year the combine was renamed Baldwins when a merger with Alfred Baldwin and Wright Butler became effective. The concern, originally formed in response to amalgamations among American rivals,[1] went on to acquire a Port Talbot bar and plate plant, owned by the German firm Siemens, from the Custodian of Enemy Property in 1915. John Lysaght acquired J. Sankey in 1919 and were themselves acquired by Guest Keen and Nettlefolds in 1920. The Grovesend Steel and Tinplate Company entered the sheet trade by acquisition in 1913, and between 1919 and 1923 acquired seven works. Then in 1923 Grovesend and Richard Thomas merged to become the third largest concern in the industry, following Summers and Lysaght. Summers probably produced about a fifth of British sheet output and Lysaght a little more than 10 per cent, while Richard Thomas–Grovesend, although with capacity to supply some 23 per cent of British requirements, probably produced about 7–8 per cent.[2]

Other firms were merger-active in the 1920s and 1930s, or had been before then, but the prospects for the installation of modern continuous or semi-continuous strip mills, which would produce sheet of the quality demanded by consumer durables industries, lay with Summers, Lysaght, Baldwins and Richard Thomas. The latter set the pace in the 1930s when, hampered by producer quotas in sheet and tinplate, it acquired nineteen sheet works between 1933 and 1936.

These purchases allowed the new Richard Thomas Ebbw Vale sheet plant to come on stream in 1937. Richard Thomas's new and old plant could supply about 50 per cent of British tinplate and sheet requirements combined, although in sheet its share was 'much smaller'.[3] John Summers, recognising the future shape of the industry, built a sheet plant at Shotton which was in operation by late 1939. Thomas and Summers together had a strip capacity of 1,100,000 tons in late 1939, whereas uncoated sheet output in 1938 was only 568,000 tons. Baldwins, too, could not isolate itself from these developments and merged with Richard Thomas in December 1944. The Steel Company of Wales (SCOW), a joint concern dominated by Richard Thomas and Baldwin (RTB) and formed in 1947, brought a third strip mill into operation at Margam, South Wales, in 1951.

The first nationalisation of the steel industry formally took effect from October 1950,[4] and the ninety-four companies acquired by the Iron and Steel Corporation of Great Britain between them controlled some 93 per cent of sheet output.[5] However, the three plants at Ebbw Vale, Shotton

---

[1] Ibid. pp. 106–7.   [2] Ibid. pp. 129–35.   [3] Ibid. p. 184.
[4] D. Burn, *The Steel Industry 1939–1959: a study in competition and planning*, Cambridge University Press, 1961, p. 311.
[5] W. Gumbel and K. Potter, *The Iron and Steel Act, 1949*, London, Butterworth, 1951, p. xiii.

and Margam produced roughly 70 per cent,[1] so that the trade would have been highly concentrated even in the absence of nationalisation. The return to power of the Conservatives in 1951 produced denationalisation by 1953; effectively, the ISHRA was set up to take over all the assets and liabilities of the Iron and Steel Corporation and to return the nationalised undertakings to private ownership.[2] Eventually all the sheet undertakings acquired in 1950 were returned to private ownership except RTB, which remained in the ISHRA until the second nationalisation episode in 1967, when it was acquired by the British Steel Corporation.

Denationalisation loosened the structure of the industry slightly but concentration was still high. Price as well as quality competition was introduced in 1954 and this quickened the demise of the older 'mechanised' and hand mills. RTB inherited some capacity from the 1950 nationalisation and acquired some old Siemens sheet works in the mid-1950s to nurse them through to closure. John Summers acquired three works from the ISHRA for the same purpose. In consequence the continuous or semi-continuous strip mills owned by RTB, Summers and the SCOW produced 74·7 per cent of British sheet in 1956 (three years after the formation of the ISHRA), 88·3 per cent in 1960 and 96·7 per cent in 1962, during which year two new strip mills commenced production.[3] Nationalisation of steel concentrated virtually all production into one concern in 1967.

In summary, mergers promoted privately or by the State have played a decisive role in increasing concentration in steel sheet. The internal growth of previously merger-active firms completed the introduction of the modern continuous production processes for which the mergers of the 1930s, 1940s and 1950s had been sought.

Tin and tin alloys

Evely and Little noted: '. . . Consolidated Tin Smelters was formed in 1929 to acquire three smelting companies, and proceeded to concentrate production at the Williams Harvey plant at Bootle. As a result of this merger, Consolidated accounted for 90 per cent of the total British production of refined tin.'[4] The concentration level in refined tin (blocks, ingots, bars and slabs) has remained substantially the same since, with the other major smelter, Capper Pass and Son, producing much of the remaining output. Indeed, a publication of the International Tin Study Group[5]

[1] Warren, *The British Iron and Steel Sheet Industry*, p. 246.

[2] B. S. Keeling and A. E. C. Wright, *The Development of the Modern British Steel Industry*, London, Longmans, 1964, p. 178.

[3] One at Llanwern for RTB and the other in Scotland for Colvilles; Warren, *The British Iron and Steel Sheet Industry*, pp. 249 and 270–81.

[4] *Concentration in British Industry*, p. 120.

[5] *Tin 1954*, The Hague, International Tin Study Group, 1955, pp. 16–17.

gave the capacities of only two British smelters – Consolidated at Bootle (40,000–50,000 tons per annum) and Capper Pass at Bristol and North Ferriby.[1] Towards the end of 1969 Consolidated opened a new tin smelter at Kirkby (35,000–40,000 tons of concentrates capacity per annum) to replace the old smelter at Bootle which was subsequently closed. Capper Pass's present capacity in refined tin is 15,000 tons per annum and it has a further 2,000 tons capacity for tin alloys. The only other producer of any importance in refined tin is Batchelor Robinson, which operated three detinning plants using tinplate scrap during the 1960s.

The fall in concentration over the period 1958–63 can be attributed to the decline in refined tin output (by 36·7 per cent) and the increasing contribution to total sales of soft solder, where twenty firms shared about 30 per cent of the sector in 1963.[2]

After 1963 there was some minor merger activity. In 1967 the Lead Industries Group added George Johnson (Birmingham), one of the few tin foil and sheet producers in the United Kingdom, to its interest in tin via Fry's Metals. RTZ acquired Capper Pass in 1967 and a half interest in Platt Metals, which produced some tin-based alloys and solders, in 1969. Both Capper Pass and Lead Industries are among the three main solder producers (the other is H. J. Enthoven and Sons), and these mergers may have brought a small increase in sales concentration.

Gramophone records

The flat disc gramophone record was introduced by Emile Berliner in 1895.[3] The first British firm in this trade (MLH 364) was the Gramophone Company which set up in London offices in 1898 and in 1907 built the 'His Master's Voice' factory. In 1917 the British branch of the American Columbia Company was registered as a private company and started to press records soon afterwards. By 1931 these two companies were the major concerns in the United Kingdom. During the trade recession of 1931–3 their combined profits fell from £1,422,090 in 1930 to £160,893 in 1931, and the merger of these two firms in 1931 may be regarded as defensive.[4] The combine was later to be renamed Electric and Musical Industries (now EMI). Other smaller companies had been started before the 1931 merger. Decca was formed in 1929 and used the plant of the Duophone Company of New Malden which it acquired in the same year. A year previously Crystalate Gramophone Record Manu-

---

[1] The latter plant was a postwar extension which doubled Capper Pass's capacity to roughly 10,000 tons per annum. The Bristol plant has now been closed.

[2] See Census of Production 1963, part 40, p. 14.

[3] L. G. Wood, 'The growth and development of the recording industry', *Journal of the Royal Society of Arts*, vol. 119, September 1971, pp. 666–77.

[4] *The British Record: the gramophone record industry's services to the nation from 1898 to the present day*, London, British Phonograph Committee, 1959, p. 35.

facturing was founded, and Crystalate acquired the Vocalion Gramophone Company in 1932, reflecting the same pressures to regroup as those which formed EMI. In 1937 Decca acquired all Crystalate record interests and plant, while shortly afterwards Crystalate went back into records in a minor way by acquiring a controlling interest in British Homophone, formed in 1921. The latter was a specialist producer of advertising records and is still extant. Oriole Records was formed in the depths of the record depression of 1931 and is still operating, having been acquired by the Columbia Broadcasting System of the United States (CBS) during the 1960s. Apart from records now produced under the CBS and Kinney labels, it thrived for long as a presser for independent record companies which had no pressing plant.

Thus by the advent of the 1939–45 war there were three dominant record producers (EMI, Decca and Oriole) and two of these were the result of a series of mergers. After the war a succession of new entrants loosened the grip of these three on the industry. Nixa Record Company was formed in 1952, Philips then entered the British industry with a gramophone record division founded in 1953, as did Deutsche Grammophon (Great Britain) a year later. Pye entered records by acquiring the new firm Nixa in 1953 and followed this by acquiring Polygon Records, another postwar entrant, in 1954. Thus, by 1958 the industry consisted of six major firms (EMI, Decca, Oriole, Pye, Philips and Deutsche Grammophon) and one or two minor firms. But EMI and Decca, the two merger-intensive firms, dominated: 'These two companies have 80 per cent of the trade, with EMI taking somewhat the larger share. Two other companies, Philips and Pye, have a further 10 per cent of the trade, while the balance is accounted for by smaller companies and imports.'[1]

Between 1958 and 1963 the sales share of the top five firms declined by 1·6 per cent from 99·0 to 97·4 per cent,[2] the result of further new entry into the industry. In 1959, Gala Records (a subsidiary of the Musical and Plastic Industries group) was launched with the use of a new pressing process.[3] The Record Society was launched in the same year, also using a new production process. Rank Records also entered in 1959, but pressing was performed contractually by Philips.[4] Not all new entrants lasted the course (Gala had discontinued by 1963 and Rank at about the same time), but new entry was sufficient to produce the small concentration decrease of 1·6 percentage points.

After 1963, CBS entered the trade by acquiring Oriole Records, and Associated Television acquired Pye Records after the 1966–7 purchase of

[1] F. D. Boggis, 'Breaking into records', *Cartel*, vol. 9, 1959, p. 54.
[2] Census of Production 1963, part 131, table 5.
[3] A. Cooke, 'They broke the record ring', *Business*, vol. 89, December 1959, pp. 78–9.
[4] Boggis, 'Breaking into records', pp. 56–7. Another small company to blossom during the period was Orlake, a subsidiary of Movitex.

Table 3.3.   *Gramophone records: market shares by numbers of records sold, 1967 and 1968*

Percentages

	Singles		Albums	
	1967	1968	1967	1968
EMI	33·5	29·9	28·5	31·6
Decca	24·3	11·6	30·2	18·5
Pye	11·9	11·4	11·4	5·3
Polydor Records	9·9	9·1	11·3	16·5
Philips	7·1	7·9	4·8	2·2
CBS	5·8	11·9	6·5	13·9
RCA	—	3·2	—	3·0
Others	7·5	15·0	7·3	9·0
Total	100·0	100·0	100·0	100·0

SOURCE: *Record Retailer* (various issues).

Pye by Philips. The only merger which increased concentration substantially, however, was that of Polydor Records (the renamed Deutsche Grammophon, owned by Siemens) and Philips, when Siemens and Philips combined their European record interests in the jointly owned Polygram concern in about 1970.[1] In fact the merger was more than a mutual exchange of corporate paper as the two firms now use the same pressing plant at Walthamstow. The Radio Corporation of America (RCA) has recently constructed a United Kingdom pressing plant in Durham and is the major new entrant since 1963.

The *Record Retailer* at one time published quarterly estimates of record companies' shares of the market, without distinction as to whether the companies had a pressing plant or not. The information for 1967–8 is shown in table 3.3. Although the independents ('others' in the table) are increasing their share of the market, no more than perhaps 3 per cent of total output is pressed by those below the top seven (now the top six because of the Polydor–Philips connection). The 1968 Census of Production[2] revealed that there were ten enterprises in the industry and a reasonable estimate of the five-firm sales concentration for 1971 is 92–3 per cent.[3]

This has been a merger-intensive industry throughout its relatively short

[1] See *Sunday Times*, 28 January 1973, p. 65.   [2] Part 75, table 5.
[3] That is, EMI and Decca with 53–4 per cent between them, CBS with 17 per cent, Philips–Polydor 15 per cent, RCA 7 per cent, and Pye, Crystalate, Orlake and one other with 7–8 per cent between them (see Economist Intelligence Unit, *Retail Business*, no. 98, April 1966 and no. 159, May 1971, and A. Vice, *The Strategy of Takeovers*, Maidenhead, McGraw-Hill, 1971, p. 84).

history and concentration is still very high, although the dominance of the two leading concerns is not so noticeable as it was during the 1950s. However, the recent pattern of motives for mergers has been somewhat different from that in the pre-war period.

Safety glass

The Monopolies Commission tells the history of this product (MLH 463).[1] Its first real growth came after the 1914–18 war when demand for automobiles expanded, and in 1931 when safety glass in cars became a legal requirement.

The early entrants to the trade were Triplex Safety Glass, which eventually made a success of production after 1922, Protectoglass, British Indestructo Glass and Triplex (Northern), set up in 1929, which was in fact 51 per cent owned by Pilkington Brothers and 49 per cent by Triplex Safety Glass. Another competitor, mainly using imported flat glass, was Lancegaye Safety Glass (1934) which, in 1936, acquired Gilt Edge Safety Glass, a Midlands competitor specialising in 'tempered' glass.[2] In time Triplex Safety Glass came to take a controlling interest in all these firms and was itself acquired by Pilkington in 1965.[3] Triplex acquired the goodwill, trademarks and plant of Protectoglass, a much smaller concern than itself, in 1933. A controlling interest in Lancegaye and Gilt Edge was acquired by 1939, after litigation concerning patents. Triplex (Northern) had become a subsidiary of Triplex Safety Glass by 1955, from which date Pilkington proceeded to build up its holding in the main company. British Indestructo Glass was acquired in 1967.

In 1966 the market shares (by sales value) for the major companies were Pilkington 6 per cent, Triplex 73 per cent (so that Pilkington's overall share was 79 per cent), British Indestructo 12 per cent, small firms (Splintex, Suntex Safety Glass Industries and Tudor Safety Glass) 5 per cent, merchant-tougheners 4 per cent.

In summary, high concentration in this product was not exclusively brought about by mergers, because Triplex was already a leading supplier.[4] But mergers were certainly an important tactic in disposing of competition; Protectoglass and others were small concerns, but Protectoglass was important enough for Triplex to come to a market-sharing agreement with it in 1932. Likewise, Lancegaye was not an insignificant competitor, in view of the persistence with which Triplex pursued litigation. British Indestructo had an important share of the British market before its

---

[1] *Report on the Supply of Flat Glass*, HC 83, London, HMSO, 1968, chaps. 3 and 5.
[2] See *Investors Chronicle*, 7 March 1936, p. 559; 1 August 1936, p. 286; 8 August 1936, p. 348.
[3] Pilkington, apart from its controlling interest in Triplex (Northern) and Triplex Safety Glass, still had independent production accounting for 6 per cent of British sales in 1967.
[4] Monopolies Commission, *Report on the Supply of Flat Glass*, para. 95.

assimilation. Finally Triplex (Northern) before incorporation in Triplex Safety Glass had 25 per cent of that company's trade under a 1929 quota arrangement.[1] These points are sufficient to establish that high concentration has resulted largely from mergers.

Asbestos cement goods

The history of this product (MLH 469) is covered by the Monopolies Commission.[2] The growth in United Kingdom output awaited the expiry of an Austrian patent for the production of asbestos cement sheet (a mixture of Portland cement and asbestos in the ratio of approximately 85:15). This monopoly was removed when the patent was revoked in 1909.[3] Four companies emerged into prominence before the 1914–18 war – Turner Brothers (which had produced asbestos goods since 1871), Bell's United Asbestos (which had similar origins to Turners), British Fibro-Cement and finally British Uralite.[4] The 1914–18 war, during which the demand for temporary buildings and substitutes for building materials gave some impetus to the trade, saw one new entrant, British Everite and Asbestolite. But after the war Bell's embarked on a programme of acquisition. They acquired a controlling interest in British Everite and Asbestolite in 1922, from which the combined divisions emerged as Bell's Poilite and Everite. The combine acquired British Fibro-Cement before, in 1928, it was itself acquired by Turner. Bowley refers to the event thus: '. . . Turner and Newall amalgamated with two other leading asbestos cement companies . . .'[5] (They were Bell's and British Fibro-Cement.) At that time, therefore, Turner–Bell's was the major firm, with only British Uralite as a competitor. To some extent, Turner Brothers were able to retain their dominance by acquisition; they purchased an asbestos cement factory at Rhoose from the Aberthaw and Bristol Channel Portland Cement Company in 1935 and, during the 1939–45 war, they acquired a small asbestos cement firm at the request of the government. However, ex-employees of Bell's were instrumental in starting production at Atlas Stone in 1929 and in the formation of the Universal Asbestos Manufacturing Company in 1930. Tunnel Cement entered the trade in 1936, but a year later came to a selling and distribution arrangement with Turner which is described in detail by the Monopolies Commission.[6]

After the war, Cape Asbestos started production of a board which competed with certain products in the classification, but which did not contain cement and was thus not classified as part of the trade.[7] However,

---

[1] Ibid. para. 92.
[2] Monopolies Commission, *Report on Asbestos and Certain Asbestos Products*.
[3] M. Bowley, *Innovations in Building Materials: an economic study*, London, Duckworth, 1960, p. 295.   [4] Ibid. p. 119.   [5] Ibid. p. 303.
[6] *Report on Asbestos*, paras. 109–15.
[7] 'Asbestolux', an all-asbestos board.

Cape Asbestos entered the trade in 1967 when it acquired Universal Asbestos; it was itself acquired by Charter Consolidated soon after. With the entry of Gleno Asbestos in 1967, there were six major companies in the sector – Turners Asbestos Cement, Cape–Universal, Tunnel Asbestos, Atlas Stone, British Uralite and Gleno Asbestos – but the leading four firms were responsible for over 92 per cent of sales (and one of these, Tunnel, still had the distribution arrangement with Turners).

In summary, mergers have promoted and maintained high concentration in the product group. This judgement is at variance with that of Evely and Little, who suggested that high concentration resulted from the small number of entrants to the trade.[1] We must give some weight to this view, but Evely and Little had to rely on the limited information contained in an official report.[2] The Monopolies Commission gives the definitive account of how concentration increased and we must prefer that source.[3]

Wallpaper

The history of this product (MLH 483) has been outlined by Evely and Little[4] and the Monopolies Commission.[5] More recent developments have been covered elsewhere.[6] Briefly, WPM was formed in 1899 by the voluntary amalgamation of thirty-one wallpaper firms. It was a merger-intensive firm throughout its existence until it was itself taken over by Reed Paper in 1965. In 1899 it claimed to produce 98 per cent of the total output of wallpaper, but there has been a downward trend in this proportion ever since. The trend was temporarily reversed by acquisitions in 1906, 1909 and 1913, and especially by the ten firms acquired in 1915. Further acquisitions of wallpaper companies took place in 1924, 1925 and 1934 (when six firms were acquired), and small companies were acquired in 1939, 1943 and 1945.

More recently, in 1961, WPM acquired its two major rivals – Smith and Walton, and K. L. Holdings. During the 1960s large conglomerates (ICI, Berger Jenson and Nicholson, Leyland Paints and Lead Industries) improved their position in wallpaper as against WPM, and the development of vinyl wall-coverings by smaller firms further limited the market dominance which WPM's acquisition policy had initially achieved.

In summary, this has been a merger-intensive trade throughout the present century. The tendency for high concentration to be eroded by the emergence of new competition has reasserted itself in the last decade.

[1] *Concentration in British Industry*, pp. 126–7.

[2] Ministry of Works, *The Distribution of Building Materials and Components*, London, HMSO, 1948.   [3] Monopolies Commission, *Report on Asbestos*, paras. 30, 32 and 33.

[4] *Concentration in British Industry*, pp. 269–73.

[5] *Report on the Supply of Wallpaper*, HC 59, London, HMSO, 1964, chap. 2.

[6] Hart, Utton and Walshe, *Mergers and Concentration in British Industry*, pp. 130–4.

INTERNAL-EXPANSION PRODUCTS

The sixteen internal-expansion products (listed in table 3.2) reached their high levels of concentration mainly as a result of the faster internal growth of some firms in the trade.

Frozen fish and frozen vegetables

These two products (MLH 214 and 218) will be dealt with together, as the largest firms in both these sectors of the frozen food industry are identical.

In the United Kingdom the industry developed largely after the second world war, during which Unilever acquired the patent rights in frosted foods from the joint owners, the General Foods Corporation of the United States and Chivers and Sons in the United Kingdom.[1] Early production started up in the plants of two Unilever subsidiaries – Batchelors Foods, and Poulton and Nöel. Then Unilever built its first frozen food 'Birdseye' factory (Clarence Birdseye is credited with the 'discovery' of quick freezing[2]) at Great Yarmouth and started operations there in 1946. A second 'Birdseye' factory was opened at Lowestoft in 1949, a third at Kirkby in 1953 and a fourth at Grimsby in 1956. That year also saw the start of British operations by the Swedish concern, Findus, also at Grimsby. Just after the war J. Lyons had launched the 'Frood' label of frozen foods. Despite the entry of these and other competitors, Unilever attained dominance in the industry as a whole, being responsible for about four fifths of industry sales in 1958.[3]

Nevertheless, there was significant new entry into the industry after the late 1950s, and this increased the intensity of competition.[4] One reaction to this increased competition was acquisition. Unilever acquired the small Tempo Frozen Foods in 1959 for its plant at Eastbourne (Tempo had no production in either of the sectors considered here). Nestlé, with no capacity in this industry, acquired a controlling interest in Findus in 1962, probably the second or third largest firm at the time. In 1963 Associated Fisheries sold its 'Eskimo' frozen food interests to the J. Lyons–Union International concern, which had the important brands 'Frood'

---

[1] See Harris and Seldon, *Advertising in Action*, pp. 256–71.

[2] Wilson, *Unilever 1945–1965*, p. 171.

[3] *Woman and the National Market: branded foods*, London, Odhams Press, 1958; cf. Harris and Seldon, *Advertising in Action*, p. 266, who give Unilever two thirds of the total market in 1961. Concentration was declining at this time according to the Census of Production.

[4] For details of numbers of firms in frozen fish see Census of Production 1958, part 10, table 4, p. 8 and 1963, part 10, table 5, p. 9; in frozen vegetables, see 1958, part 14, table 4, p. 7 and 1963, part 14, table 5, p. 8. On competition, see 'The shopkeepers frozen assets', *FBI Review*, October 1964, pp. 57–61.

Table 3.4. *Frozen food: manufacturers' shares of consumer sales, 1969*

Percentages

	Vegetables	Fish
Unilever	66	70
Nestlé–Lyons (Findus)	18	18
Imperial Tobacco	10	6
Others	6	6
Total	100	100

SOURCE: trade estimates.

and 'Fropax' and had been merged in early 1963. No further important acquisitions occurred until January 1968, when Nestlé's Findus was merged with the Lyons–Union concern. The combine dropped all the brand names apart from Findus, and Union's interest was sold to Lyons, so that Findus is now jointly owned by Nestlé and Lyons.

Imperial Tobacco, as part of its diversification programme, acquired National Canning in 1968, together with its Smedley's subsidiary, and, in 1969, took over the Ross Group, with its own plant and the Young's Seafoods subsidiary. Thus, by 1969, three concerns dominated the frozen foods industry in general and the fish and vegetable sectors in particular. Their shares were roughly as shown in table 3.4.

One source lists only four important firms apart from the leading three: two in vegetables (Baird Wolton and May, and Jus-Rol) and two in fish (Scottish Salmon and White Fish, and Ulster Fresh Fish).[1] Economies of scale appear to have been one motive in seeking large size,[2] while Unilever's expertise in distribution has apparently been envied by its competitors.[3]

In summary, although the lead built up by Unilever owes very little to external growth, this dominance has been whittled away by other large firms which have sought external growth as the *sine qua non* of mounting a challenge to Unilever's leadership. These mergers have undoubtedly contributed to the maintenance of high concentration in both subsectors of the industry considered here. The top three in 1969 were composed of at least eight firms which were independent in 1958.

[1] International Trade Centre, *Western European Markets for Frozen Foods*, Geneva, UNCTAD/GATT, 1969, annex II.
[2] Cf. Harris and Seldon, *Advertising in Action*, pp. 266–7; and *Financial Times*, 10 December 1971, p. 15.
[3] See K. van Musschenbroek, 'The strange levitation of Lyons', *Management Today*, May 1970, pp. 86–93.

Condensed and evaporated milk

In this country the manufacture of condensed milk (MLH 215) started in 1873 when Anglo-Swiss Condensed Milk opened plants at Chippenham and Aylesbury. Further plants were added at Middlewich (1874), Staverton (1897) and Tutbury (1901). Then, in 1905, Anglo-Swiss merged with a firm owned by Nestlé of Switzerland. It is not clear, but it seems unlikely from the evidence, that Nestlé had established any British plants by that time. Thus the pre-eminent position of Nestlé–Anglo Swiss in the British industry was largely the result of internal growth.[1]

This indeed set the pattern for expansion of all but one or two of the later entrants to the industry. In 1914 Nestlé acquired Fussell and Company, a small condensing concern founded at Salisbury in 1912, whose production, in common with the other British manufacturers, could not compare with the lead established by Nestlé. Indeed not until the 1930s did the British industry begin to supply more than a minor portion of the market. In 1919 home supplies could claim just over 31 per cent of the market,[2] while by 1924 this had fallen to 28 per cent.[3] Even by 1937 the British industry still supplied only 51 per cent of marketed condensed milk.[4]

Almost all the later entrants to the trade had dairy connections and diversified into manufactured milk products. Cow and Gate expanded over the decade 1929–39 by acquiring a number of creameries, but did not obtain any noteworthy condensing capacity. In 1929 Express Dairy acquired the West Park Dairy, which owned a creamery with condensing facilities at Frome. The Wilts United Dairies merged with two other dairies in 1915. Wilts United started condensed milk production in 1902 and had doubled capacity (to about forty employees) by 1906; a second plant was opened in 1912. The 1915 tripartite merger did not expand its interest significantly, but in the early 1930s the concern acquired the United Creameries in Scotland, which owned a small condensing plant. At about this time, too, the CWS entered the trade by acquiring a number of dairies and milk product factories, but it was still small by the outbreak of war.[5]

---

[1] Further plants were added – at Salisbury and Ashbourne in 1913, at Carlisle in 1928, at Ballymoney in 1938, at Dunragit in 1941 and at Omagh in 1942.

[2] Department of Scientific and Industrial Research, *Special Report No. 13. Studies in Sweetened and Unsweetened (Evaporated) Condensed Milk* by W. G. Savage and R. F. Hunwicke, London, HMSO, 1923, pp. 1–2.

[3] L. A. Allen, 'The Properties of Milk in relation to the Condensing and Drying of Whole Milk, Separated Milk and Whey', *Bulletin of the Hannah Dairy Research Institute*, no. 3, 1932, p. v.

[4] Imperial Economic Committee, *A Survey of the Trade in Canned Food*, London, HMSO, 1939, p. 157; this ignores the supply of condensed milk produced and used internally by chocolate manufacturers, notably Cadbury.

[5] P. Redfern, *The New History of the CWS*, London, J. M. Dent, 1938, p. 548, where the CWS is said to have had fourteen milk product factories – making butter, cheese, etc., as well as condensed milk – with, however, a *total* of only eighty-three employees.

However, the most important entrants to the trade arrived after the setting up of the Milk Marketing Board in 1933.[1] Both Carnation Foods and Libby McNeill and Libby set up plant in the United Kingdom in 1935. At that time, Nestlé, Carnation and Libby were the major suppliers to the British market, the last two through imports. Carnation set up a seasonal packing operation at Dumfries in Scotland, canning the whole year's supply in about two thirds of the year. This decision, borrowed from American practice, stood them in good stead during the 1939–45 war, when demand expanded dramatically and other manufacturers found it difficult to acquire new plant. Neither Carnation nor Libby have made any acquisitions in the sector, so that, like Nestlé, they owe their position in the trade to internal growth.

These three concerns supplied 90 per cent or more of the condensed and evaporated milk sold on the household market in 1958 and about 83 per cent of all supplies in 1968.[2] They have substantial shares in the catering and manufacturing markets, although there CWS and the dairies are more in evidence. The merger of Cow and Gate and United Dairies in 1959 to become Unigate, and the acquisition of Minsterley Creameries by Express Dairy in 1959, were probably responsible for the small increase in concentration of sales among the top five concerns between 1958 and 1963. Unigate, partly through subsequent acquisitions, has gone on to expand its interest in this sector.[3]

In summary, mergers have played but a minor role in establishing three or four producers as pre-eminent in this trade. While the dairy companies have expanded consistently by mergers, the evidence indicates that the condensing capacity acquired did not give them large shares in the market.

Ice cream

Evely and Little concluded that acquisition had played no part in the growth of Unilever and Lyons to leadership in the ice cream trade (MLH 215).[4] One source gave the following shares of the retail market to Unilever and Lyons in 1968: Unilever (Walls, Mr Whippy) 62 per cent, J. Lyons (Lyons Maid, Eldorado, Neilson, Mr Softee) 24 per cent, others 14 per cent.[5] Thus, concentration, allowing for the fact that the survey did not encompass non-retail buyers, seems likely to have remained high.

The 1963 Census of Production registered only a very small increase in

[1] This is taken as a significant date by W. C. Harvey and H. Hill, *Milk Products*, London, H. K. Lewis, 1948, p. 227.

[2] Cf. Economist Intelligence Unit, *Retail Business*, no. 123, May 1968, p. 61.

[3] Variously estimated to lie between 7 and 16 per cent of British output.

[4] *Concentration in British Industry*, p. 125.

[5] *Woman and the National Market: branded foods*.

concentration for a period when significant merger activity took place.[1] In the late 1950s Unilever's ice cream subsidiary, T. Wall and Sons (Ice Cream), expanded into the 'soft' ice cream business (using machines capable of producing soft ice cream installed in mobile vans). In 1963 that side of the business was merged with Forte's 'Mr Whippy'. Then in 1966 Unilever acquired Forte's interest in the combined operation (which at first controlled 1800 vans).

In the mid-1950s Neilsons (Holdings) was formed, with two ice cream subsidiaries, and proceeded to acquire a number of small concerns. J. Lyons acquired Neilsons in 1962 and merged its ice cream interests with the Union International subsidiary, Eldorado Ice Cream, which was at that time probably the fourth largest firm in the British trade. By 1970, J. Lyons had bought out the Union International share of the operating company, Glacier Foods, which was set up to operate the Lyons–Neilson–Eldorado combine. Lyons also went on to acquire Bertorelli's (Ice Cream), and in 1969 it bought Tonibell Manufacturing from British-American Tobacco.

In 1963 a much smaller company in the trade, Unigate, acquired the Midland Counties Dairy, which had a minor ice cream interest. But in 1967 Northern Dairies, which has about 70–80 per cent of the Northern Ireland market, sold its English and Welsh ice cream plant to Unigate–Midland. Then, in 1972, Unigate sold its accumulated interests in ice cream to Lyons.

Thus, in summary, high concentration was not initially the result of merger activity. However, in the period 1958–63 a new system of trading (by mobile van, selling soft ice cream) both offered the prospect of growth and threatened to erode the leaders' shares. Subsequently, Unilever and Lyons have acquired the most important new entrants. This reaction, and other acquisitions which do not fit that pattern, have maintained high concentration. But the existence of some 2000 small manufacturers serving isolated local markets must be noted in assessing the effects of mergers on the structure of the trade.[2]

Soups

The birth of a substantial soup industry (MLH 218) can be traced back to before the 1940s,[3] but certainly the last vestiges of consumer resistance to tinned soups were eliminated by wartime conditions. Soup was first tinned in Great Britain by specialist firms: Donkin Hall and Gamble in

---

[1] National Board for Prices and Incomes, *Report No. 160. Costs, Prices and Profitability in the Ice Cream Manufacturing Industry*, Cmnd 4548, London, HMSO, 1970, especially the appendix.

[2] Ibid. para. 1. Because most of these local firms have less than twenty-five employees their sales are not included in the denominator of the concentration ratio.

[3] Cf. *Food Processing and Packaging*, December 1964, p. 479.

the 1810s (for sailors and explorers); John Lusty with turtle soup in 1862;[1] Poulton and Nöel during the Boer war; and W. Symington with packeted powder soups at the turn of the century.

These and other firms survived into the present century, when they were joined by other food preservers such as Crosse and Blackwell,[2] Bender and Cassel, and W. A. Baxter and Sons. The 1914–18 war broke down some of the resistance to tinned foods, while developments in production of tins for this purpose set the scene for later expansion. In 1930, H. J. Heinz introduced its first range of soups.[3] In 1933, the CWS first packed soups at Lowestoft[4] and, in the same year, Unilever moved Poulton and Nöel production into one of its old margarine plants at Southall. Batchelors Foods, which had established itself as market leader in tinned peas, first tinned soup in 1937.

During the 1939–45 war, Heinz established itself as the market leader, and in 1951 it is said to have made 70,000 tons of soup,[5] while the 1951 Census of Production reveals that large establishments produced a total of 79,400 tons of soup in that year. In 1943, Unilever acquired Batchelors who, with Crosse and Blackwell and the CWS, constituted the only substantial competition to Heinz. Thus the merger of Unilever's two interests in soup did not contribute significantly to high concentration.

The first challenge to Heinz leadership in soup came in 1951, when Batchelors launched a dehydrated soup. The second challenge came from the internal growth of Campbell's Soups.[6]

Batchelors were joined a few years later by Maggi, a Nestlé subsidiary, and Knorr Anglo-Swiss, which changed hands a number of times until it was acquired by the American concern, Corn Products, in 1960. The share of packeted soups in total market value increased from 10 per cent in 1957 to 24 per cent in 1969.[7] Knorr steadily expanded its share of the packet soup market, claiming three fifths of sector sales in 1961, while Batchelors made 20 per cent and Maggi 7 per cent.[8] However, by 1969 Batchelors had regained lost ground and could claim 49 per cent of market value, Knorr having 21 per cent and Maggi 13·4 per cent (with much of the remainder going to own-label brands manufactured by these three leaders).

[1] *Self Service and Supermarket*, 6 January 1972.
[2] Crosse and Blackwell was a 1920 combine of general 'food preservers' (P. Fitzgerald, *Industrial Combination in England* (2nd ed.), London, Pitman, 1927).
[3] Heinz had started food manufacture in Great Britain with the purchase of Battys, a pickle packing plant at Peckham, in 1905 (see S. Potter, *The Magic Number, the Story of '57'*, London, Reinhardt, 1959, p. 109).
[4] Redfern, *The New History of the CWS*, p. 353.
[5] *Grocers' Gazette*, 15 November 1958.
[6] A new entrant in 1959 – see for background *Grocers' Gazette*, 20 May 1961; *Business*, vol. 93, September 1963, pp. 58ff.; *Management Today*, September 1967, pp. 100–3.
[7] *Grocer*, 4 October 1969.   [8] *Financial Times*, 18 February 1961.

Nestlé's Maggi interest was joined by the Crosse and Blackwell products in 1960, when Nestlé acquired the latter. Crosse and Blackwell at that time could claim about 20 per cent of tinned soup sales, Heinz having 61 per cent and Campbell's Soups 13 per cent.[1] Thus, Crosse and Blackwell were one of the top five producers, and the addition of Maggi contributed to the concentration increase between 1958 and 1963.

The packet soup firms have, by capturing a larger share of the overall market, eroded Heinz leadership very slightly.[2] Nevertheless, concentration has remained high because Heinz's losses have been the gains of only a few competitors. In the second half of the 1960s overall market shares (tinned and dry soups) of the top five producers summed to roughly 92 per cent.[3]

In summary, mergers have occurred in this trade but have contributed very little to oligopolisation. High concentration came about through the internal growth of Heinz and has since been eroded by only three substantial competitors.

Coffee extracts and essences

By 1958 soluble powder coffee accounted for roughly 79 per cent of the coffee produced by large firms, and the corresponding figure for 1963 was 89 per cent.[4] Ground coffee was excluded from this product group (MLH 229) in both 1958 and 1963; liquid coffee (or coffee and chicory) essences were the remaining outputs of the sector.

Before the 1939–45 war liquid coffee claimed some 70 per cent of the market and the rest was taken by varieties of ground coffee.[5] Chief among the liquid coffee firms was R. Paterson and Sons with 'Camp', followed by J. Lyons' 'Bev', Brooke Bond's 'Bon' and the CWS brand 'Shield Hall'. Paterson started making 'Camp' in 1885 and by 1906 it was their sole product. In 1939 Nestlé introduced the first successful soluble powdered coffee, Nescafé, and its 'convenience' appeal ensured rapid growth of sales after the end of hostilities (just as had occurred with 'Camp' after the 1914–18 war). By 1950 Nescafé supplied 100 per cent of what had come to be known as the 'instant' coffee market. 'Nu-caf' from the CWS and 'Quoffy' from Lyons tried to challenge Nescafé in the early

---

[1] Ibid.

[2] Meanwhile, in its chosen field, tinned soup, Heinz has increased its share; Campbell's and Crosse and Blackwell have lost shares in this market over the period 1961–71. Also, new tinned soups were launched by CPC (UK) and Ranks Hovis McDougall in the late 1960s and early 1970s.

[3] Heinz 54 per cent, Nestlé 14 per cent, Batchelors 10 per cent, Campbell's 9 per cent, Knorr 5 per cent (see *Grocer*, 21 August 1965 and 4 October 1969).

[4] Census of Production 1963, part 17, p. 97.

[5] Harris and Seldon, *Advertising in Action*, pp. 168–74.

Table 3.5. *Instant coffee: market shares by numbers of drinkers, 1958–68*

Percentages

	1958	1963	1968
Nescafé	76	57	55
Maxwell House	14	22	26
Others	10	21	19
Total	100	100	100

SOURCE: *Woman and the National Market.*

years but were soon withdrawn. By 1954, instant coffee accounted for 35 per cent of market sales, liquid coffee for 40 per cent and ground coffee for the remaining 25 per cent. At this point the General Foods Corporation of the United States entered the market with imports of 'Maxwell House' and two years later set up British processing plant.[1]

The concentration of sales among the top five producers was 97·9 per cent in 1958 and 98·4 per cent in 1963. Estimates of shares of the major brands in the instant coffee sector are shown in table 3·5·

In addition, General Foods supplied a number of retailers with coffee powder for their own labels and these were of increasing importance over the years 1960–3.[2] The third largest firm at present is Sol Café. This was a subsidiary of the Chock Ful O'Nuts Corporation of the United States, but was acquired by J. Lyons over the period 1965–8. Sol Café, using Lyons' processing plant, specialises in supplying retailers in the own-label sector;[3] it is now estimated to supply about 80 per cent of the own-label market.[4]

This is the only merger worth mentioning in the history of the product. But it did not increase concentration of production because Sol Café was only a packing unit before being acquired by Lyons. Brooke Bond has accumulated a number of subsidiaries in the coffee field generally,[5] but in fact produces coffee only in the small liquid sector and buys in its supply of powder coffee. One source estimates the following market shares for all coffee in 1968: Nestlé 50 per cent, General Foods 27 per cent, J. Lyons 17 per cent, others 3 per cent, and imports 3 per cent.[6] But this probably does not take account of the liquid essence sector which, although

---

[1] Ibid. p. 170.   [2] *FBI Review*, June 1964, pp. 40–1.

[3] Up to the time of the connection with Lyons, Sol Café had no processing plant in this country and was purely a marketing company.

[4] *Management Today*, May 1970.

[5] Priory Tea and Coffee, Kenna Coffee, English Chicory, Mabroukie Tea and Coffee.

[6] International Trade Centre, *Twenty one European Markets for Industrial Coffee*, Geneva, UNCTAD/GATT, 1969.

small, is still dominated by 'Camp'; this brand has always had over half of liquid coffee sales in the postwar period.

In summary, mergers have played no role in the achievement of high concentration in the trade. The product superiority enjoyed by a few firms has been sufficient to limit the market shares obtained by new entrants.

Synthetic rubber

Synthetic rubber (MLH 271) was first produced in the years 1908–10 by a British company, but the costs and inferior quality forbad commercial development. A ready supply of natural rubber discouraged further research in the United Kingdom, but it proceeded apace in the United States and Germany. After the second world war, the price stability of synthetic rubber, its practical advantages (for example, resistance to oil and extreme conditions) and improvements in the quality of the product, encouraged manufacturers to press for a government-sponsored synthetic rubber industry such as existed in the United States and Germany.[1] But because the basic materials of synthetic rubber are styrene and butadiene (petroleum chemicals derived from gases released during the catalytic cracking of crude oil), the creation of large plants had to wait until the oil refining industry had expanded in the decade after 1945. The first synthetic rubber plants produced small quantities of specialised rubbers, and general purpose synthetic rubber was mainly imported from firms such as Du Pont. International Synthetic Rubber, formed in 1956 by the major tyre manufacturers – Dunlop (45 per cent of equity), Firestone Tyre and Rubber, Goodyear Tyre and Rubber, Avon Rubber, Michelin Tyre, Pirelli, North British Rubber (now Uniroyal) and British Tyre and Rubber – was the first large-scale producer. Other much smaller plants were operated by British Geon (a subsidiary of Distillers) and Midland Silicones (a Dow Corning–Albright and Wilson subsidiary). Du Pont, which previously exported synthetic rubber to the United Kingdom, built a plant in Londonderry, and British petrochemical companies such as BP Chemicals (UK) and Esso Chemical began to build plants.

In 1958, the British industry still supplied only 17·3 per cent of British consumption, while by 1964 the figure was 92·3 per cent and in 1968 the United Kingdom was self-sufficient.[2] The major producer in Great Britain is International Synthetic Rubber, which had a plant with an annual capacity of 50,000 tons on stream in 1958,[3] while the Census of Production

---

[1] See A. G. Donnithorne, *British Rubber Manufacturing: an economic study of innovations*, London, Duckworth, 1958, pp. 27–34.
[2] *Not from Trees Alone: the story of synthetic rubber* (2nd ed.), London, British Association of Synthetic Rubber Manufacturers, 1970, fig. 6, p. 68.
[3] Ibid. p. 17.

Table 3.6. *Synthetic rubber and latex: United Kingdom capacity, 1970 and planned*

	Location of plant	Capacity		Planned capacity
		Volume	Proportion of total	
		(long tons)	(%)	(long tons)
BP Chemicals (UK)	Barry	12,000	2·9	12,000
Doverstrand	Stallingborough	25,000	6·1	35,000
Dow Chemical	Kings Lynn	6,000	1·5	15,000
Du Pont	Londonderry	30,000	7·4	60,000
Dunlop	Birmingham	10,500	2·6	12,500
Esso Chemical	Fawley	36,000	8·8	44,000
International Synthetic Rubber	Grangemouth (I)	80,000	} 64·5	80,000
	Grangemouth (II)	3,000		15,000
	Hythe (I)	180,000		180,000
	Hythe (II)	—		30,000
Marbon Chemical	Grangemouth	10,000	2·5	10,000
Uniroyal	Stoke Prior	15,000	3·7	15,000
Total		407,500	100·0	508,500

SOURCE: *Not from Trees Alone*, p. 13.

for 1958 implies a quantity of sales by larger firms in the region of 10,000 tons.[1] That year, thirteen enterprises reported sales of synthetic rubber. Production by larger firms reported in the Census of Production for 1963 was 122,000 tons and nine enterprises reported sales. The five-firm concentration ratio had increased from 91·7 to 99·4 per cent. That concentration should increase in such a rapidly expanding trade is probably explained by limits to the economic size of plant.[2] Some small firms, or the small plants of large firms, certainly left the industry during the period 1958–63, leaving the field open to the large firms – chief of which was International Synthetic Rubber, whose capacity in 1964 equalled just under 80 per cent of British production.

Since 1963, as table 3.6 indicates, concentration has probably reverted to the 1958 level as the other manufacturers have caught up with International Synthetic Rubber and a major new entrant[3] has expanded production. There was some concentration of ownership when British Petroleum acquired Distillers' chemical interests, including their jointly owned concern, British Geon.

[1] Part 28, table 5.
[2] Cf. *Not from Trees Alone*, p. 60: '. . . the minimum economic size of a plant which can be built for the manufacture of general purpose synthetic rubber is now not less than 100,000 tons a year.'
[3] Doverstrand, a subsidiary of Revertex Holdings.

In summary, high concentration in this trade resulted from the collaboration of tyremakers in the establishment of one large firm which produced the major proportion of British supplies. Although concentration has probably declined somewhat from the level recorded in 1963, plant scale-economies promise to maintain a highly concentrated structure in the trade.

Fish and marine animal oils

Since 1948 the total physical output of this product (MLH 275(1)) as shown in the Census of Production has declined, although some individual oils have prospered. Total sales were only £2·2 million in 1951, when the supply of most oils was still under government control, and much of the sales value attributed to the sector was in fact processing work performed for the Ministry of Food. Since decontrol, sales value has naturally increased; but this is still a small trade, with sales in 1958 of £9·8 million and in 1963 of £12·0 million. Thus, in 1963 sales were just above the threshold level for estimation of the concentration ratio.

Historically, whale oil has been the major product in the census group. Its share in total sales was 68 per cent in 1934, fluctuated between 53 per cent and 72 per cent in subsequent census years, and fell precipitately to 21 per cent in 1963 (from 72 per cent in 1958). By 1963, cod liver oils (30·6 per cent) and non-whale fish body oils (38·9 per cent) were of greater relative importance.

Unilever's interest in whaling and whale oils stretches back to before the 1914–18 war.[1] In 1917 the government took over the distribution of whale oil in the United Kingdom and allocated it as follows: Lever Brothers 47·4 per cent (later 40 per cent), Joseph Crosfield and Sons 31·6 per cent (later 35 per cent), Olympia Oil and Cake 21·0 per cent (later 25 per cent).[2] Lever Brothers attempted to acquire Olympia Oil and Cake in 1919, but were outbid by a rival margarine concern, Jurgens. A well-known series of mergers culminated in the late 1920s with Jurgens and Lever as parts of Unilever (with Crosfield earlier acquired by Lever). However, Procter and Gamble, and Kraft are two of a number of firms which entered this market after the formation of Unilever. There is clearly an imbalance between the economic size of a whale oil refining plant and the shares of the soap and margarine markets supplied by these firms. Eventually, in 1964, as the demands of the whaling nations had outrun the fecundity of the species, Christian Salvesen, from whom Unilever had purchased unrefined whale oils, sold off the last British whaler to a

---

[1] See C. Wilson, *The History of Unilever: a study in economic growth and social change*, London, Cassell, 1954, vol. 1, p. 239; Gavin Maxwell, 'Whaling', *Progress*, no. 238, Spring 1953, pp. 70ff.; 'Antarctic harvest', *Unilever International*, Spring 1964.

[2] Wilson, *The History of Unilever*, p. 239.

Japanese concern. Since then, refined whale oil has become an insignificant proportion of fish body oils supplied to the market.[1]

The slack on the market was taken up by non-whale fish body oils. Procter and Gamble, the soap manufacturers, have recently started to sell quantities of refined fish body oils to other users, as once they sold quantities of refined whale oil. The bulk of refined fish body oils emanates from two Liverpool firms – Peerless Refining (Liverpool) and Liverpool Central Oil – one Glaswegian concern – Clyde Oil Extraction – and Marfleet Refining in Yorkshire. All of these firms are subsidiaries of larger concerns which regard fish oils as incidental to their main business, and none of the firms involved has acquired other fish oil refiners.

The United Kingdom has always been one of the largest producers of fish liver oils.[2] Virtually all British sales may be attributed to one firm, Associated Fisheries, which controls Marfleet Refining, operators of the largest cod liver oil refinery in the world.[3] Marfleet Refining was founded as a joint company set up by a large number of Hull and Grimsby trawler owners.[4] As these latter were gradually acquired by Associated Fisheries, so Marfleet was gradually acquired and control was achieved early in 1964. Because Associated Fisheries had no previous refining interest, this acquisition did not increase concentration in the trade.

The unrefined oil sector is very small and dominated by three British concerns, Herring By-Products, Hull Fish Meal and Oil, and Grimsby Fish Meal. Two of these firms have acquired other concerns during the 1960s. In 1970 Herring By-Products acquired a reduction plant at Stornoway from the Herring Industry Board,[5] and Hull Fish Meal and Oil acquired North Shields Fish-Meal and Oil in the late 1960s. The greater proportion of unrefined fish oils used by the refining sector is imported.

In summary, whether one classifies this product as growing externally or internally depends on one's view as to Unilever's importance. Certainly,

[1] Ministry of Agriculture, Fisheries and Food statistical releases show that total production (*not* market sales) of refined fish body oils in 1968 was whale oil 6·9 thousand tons, herring oil 131·1 thousand tons, others 90·4 thousand tons. Sales of 32·7 thousand tons of refined whale oil are recorded for 1963 in the 1963 Census of Production.

[2] Commonwealth Economic Committee, *Report 41. Fish*, London, HMSO, 1966, paras. 192–4, shows that the British share of world production was 31 per cent in 1964.

[3] H. Rees, *Industries of Britain*, London, Harrap, 1970, p. 55: '... with an annual output of twelve to fifteen thousand tons ...'

[4] Grimsby Fishing Vessel Owners' Association, *Grimsby: the world's premier fishing port*, London, Burrow, 1959, pp. 97ff., claims that Hull and Grimsby together produced half the world production of cod liver oil.

[5] See Ministry of Agriculture, Fisheries and Food. *Report of the Committee of Enquiry into the Fishing Industry*, Cmnd 1266, London, HMSO, 1961, para. 38. The Herring Industry Board set up meal and oil reduction plants before and after the war, but these were gradually closed, or sold to private interests, as uneconomic; the Board supplied less than 1 per cent of total trade sales in 1958 and 1963.

at present, this is minor as regards refined fish oils. While this has not always been the case, it may be doubted whether Unilever has ever made much more than 40–5 per cent of total sales, requiring much of its production for its own use, as did Kraft, Procter and Gamble, and the CWS.[1] That being so, we may properly conclude that high concentration in the trade results from the fact that few firms have ever entered it.

Detergents

The history of this product (MLH 275(2)) is summarised by the Monopolies Commission.[2] After 1945 Procter and Gamble introduced 'Freedom', a dish washing powder, and 'Dreft', a light duty synthetic powder (which had made a brief appearance before the war). These were quickly followed by Unilever's 'Wisk', a heavy duty clothes powder, and 'Quix', a washing up liquid. The CWS and Colgate-Palmolive marketed synthetic powders, manufactured by Marchon Products, soon after the two leaders.[3] Synthetic powders and liquids had just 18 and 7 per cent respectively of the market in 1950, but after the introduction of 'Tide' by Procter and Gamble in that year, 'the first heavy duty synthetic powder with washing power comparable with that of the best soap powders',[4] synthetics rapidly increased their share. Unilever responded by introducing 'Surf' in 1952; 'Spel', the Marchon Products version marketed by the CWS, came out in the same year. By 1966, synthetic powders and liquids represented 39 and 19 per cent of all detergent sales.

Mergers have been of scant importance in the short history of the trade. Unilever acquired Pinoya Holdings in 1961, which owned Domestos, probably the third largest liquid detergent firm at that time.[5] Again in 1967, Unilever acquired Alcock (Peroxide), which had an interest in industrial detergents. But neither of these acquisitions gave Unilever a large increase in market share. The market shares of participants in 1964–5 were, roughly, Unilever 34·5 per cent, Procter and Gamble 50·4 per cent and others 15·1 per cent.[6] Sales of 'Stergene' and 'Squezy' (both acquired from Pinoya) gave Unilever an additional 5·9 per cent of the market in 1964. Procter and Gamble has never acquired any of its competitors in this field and, although some small liquid detergent makers may have joined forces, none of the more important smaller firms has acquired

---

[1] For example, in 1958 when refined whale oil constituted some 72 per cent of sales in the sector, seven enterprises made sales of refined whale oil.

[2] *Household Detergents*, chaps. 2 and 3.

[3] Marchon Products was acquired by Albright and Wilson in 1955.

[4] Monopolies Commission, *Household Detergents*, para. 14.

[5] See Hart, Utton and Walshe, *Mergers and Concentration in British Industry*, pp. 87–8, for more details.

[6] Monopolies Commission, *Household Detergents*, para. 25.

capacity (CWS, Colgate-Palmolive, Marchon Products, P.C. Products (1001), Three Hands Products, Thawpit, BP Detergents).

In summary, domination of this trade by a few firms has been largely achieved by means other than mergers. The Monopolies Commission argued that heavy advertising had erected high entry barriers to the trade,[1] but this view has been questioned.[2]

Crawler tractors

The first crawler or tracklaying tractor to operate successfully was built in California in 1904 by a Mr Holt. His concern merged with that of a rival in 1925 and the combine, eventually named Caterpillar Tractor, came to dominate world production of crawler tractors.[3] In Great Britain, however, crawler tractors (MLH 336) were established in production rather late. Firms such as Bristol Tractors and John Fowler (Leeds) were among the early entrants, while Ford, established at Dagenham in 1933, eventually added crawlers to its range of popular wheeled tractors.

After the 1939–45 war, one source stated that John Fowler were 'the only makers of heavy agricultural crawlers'[4] and, because of diversion to military production it is probable that Fowler and Ford were the only makers during the war. The sellers' market after the war encouraged a number of new entrants, both in the agricultural and construction equipment sectors. Table 3.7 gives the names of producers and the numbers of models they produced in the United Kingdom in 1955 and 1962. Fowler, International Harvester, Bristol Tractors, David Brown Tractors and County Commercial Cars were probably the leading five manufacturers in 1958, sharing 90·1 per cent of total sales, while the remaining six manufacturers shared under 10 per cent.[5]

By 1963 the leading five manufacturers shared 98·0 per cent of sales and five other makers shared 2 per cent.[6] This increase in concentration, in what was already a highly concentrated trade, was caused by the entry of new producers and the exit of, presumably, less efficient producers. In 1958 Caterpillar Tractor produced its first crawler tractors in the United Kingdom at Glasgow[7] and, with the technical superiority of its products,

[1] Ibid. passim.

[2] G. Polanyi, *Detergents: a question of monopoly?*, London, Institute of Economic Affairs, 1970.

[3] G. Barber, 'How mechanised building aids have evolved', *Plant Hire*, vol. 3, July 1965, pp. 26ff.

[4] *Agricultural Machinery: a report on the industry*, London, Political and Economic Planning, 1949, p. 12. Fowlers were acquired in 1947 by Marshall Sons, a wheeled tractor maker, which was in turn acquired by Thos. W. Ward in the late 1960s.

[5] In 1958 there were still only eleven manufacturers – Census of Production 1958, part 47, p. 6.

[6] Also in 1958, two of the smallest six manufacturers shared roughly 8 per cent of sales, leaving 2 per cent among four firms – Census of Production 1963, part 131, table 5.

[7] Caterpillar already had a spares plant depot at Leicester and in 1956 had acquired Birtley Iron, whose plant it rebuilt and opened in 1962 to make equipment for mounting on crawlers.

Table 3.7.   *Crawler tractors: models produced in the United Kingdom, 1955 and 1962*

	1955	1962
Albion Motors	1	—
Atkinson Hacker Tractor	4	—
Bristol Tractors	2	1
David Brown Tractors	3	2
J. I. Case	—	1
Caterpillar Tractor	—	2
County Commercial Cars	3	3
James A. Cuthbertson	—	1
Ford Motor	3	—
General Motors Scotland–Euclid (GB)	—	1
International Harvester	2	3
Marshall Sons–John Fowler (Leeds)	4	3
Ransomes Sims and Jefferies	2	1
Rotary Hoes	3	—
Vickers	1	—

SOURCE: *Directory of Wheel and Track-Type Tractors produced throughout the World, 1955* and *1962,* Rome, Food and Agriculture Organization.

quickly established market leadership in the higher horse-power construction models.[1] The second major new entrant of the period 1958–63 was another American concern, J. I. Case, which was first registered as a private company in 1960 and started producing at Pudsey in 1961. The Case models had a transmission system which performed better than most existing British makes under wet boggy conditions.[2] Since 1963, both Massey-Ferguson Holdings and Allis-Chalmers Manufacturing, established in wheeled tractors, have entered the crawler tractor sector in a small way, but the number of firms in the industry is still not large.

In summary, a spate of new entry to the sector, which continued into the 1960s, decreased concentration post-1945. However, certain of the new entrants, especially the American concerns with a technological lead over British producers, quickly established large shares of the market, so that the increase in concentration over the period 1958–63 in fact signified successful new competition being offered to established concerns, some of which were forced out of the industry.

[1] Similarly, from 1952 International Harvester had been able to promote their lower horse-power crawlers because of a technically advanced bucket attachment.
[2] A third entrant after 1955 was General Motors Scotland, which had merged with the Euclid Organisation in 1953 and brought out one high horse-power crawler in the late 1950s. The range was doubled in 1967 and trebled slightly later.

Ball and roller bearings

For the most part, the largest companies in this product (MLH 349) have grown internally. Their establishment in this country can be traced either to the ownership of foreign patents, or to the 1914–18 war when foreign bearings were virtually unobtainable and government promotion of manufacture took place.

Hoffmann Manufacturing was founded in Chelmsford in 1898, having acquired American patents for the manufacture of steel balls; the Skefko Ball Bearing Company built its first factory at Luton in 1911, introducing the processes of the parent company in Sweden; British Timken, established in 1909 in Birmingham, imported the technology of its parent, Timken Roller Bearing of Ohio. Ransome and Marles Bearing Company was first formed in 1917 to increase bearing production for the war effort, although A. Ransome had been supplying bearings to industry in a small way for some years previously. G.L. Manufacturing (later to become Pollard Ball and Roller Bearing) was first registered in 1919.[1]

Other smaller companies were established after the 1914–18 war, notably Fischer Bearings, a subsidiary of a German concern, in 1936. But the five firms which had been established by 1919 grew to pre-eminence in the trade. Skefko expanded the Luton plant, until another plant was established at Sundon in 1939 and a third at Irvine in 1962; through these plants Skefko claimed about a quarter of the United Kingdom market in the late 1960s.[2] The need to establish mass production units drove Ransome and Marles to open new plant at Annfield Plain in 1953. Expansion by Hoffmann led them to open another factory at Stonehouse in 1939. British Timken and Pollard have both expanded partly by acquisition; the former acquired Fischer Bearings from the Custodian of Enemy Property in 1940, but in 1960 this interest was sold off to an American company.[3] Apart from this, British Timken expanded with new plants in Northamptonshire in 1941 and 1954. The only permanent addition to capacity by merger was achieved by Pollard which, after a number of expansions on different sites, acquired Hanwell Engineering in 1957. At the time of the purchase the entire Hanwell output of bearings was sold to Pollard.[4]

More recently, this highly concentrated trade has become even more concentrated through the agency of the IRC. The IRC's operations during 1968–9 brought Ransome and Marles, Hoffmann and Pollard

---

[1] It is probable that G.L. did not at first manufacture bearings.

[2] Ministry of Technology, *Industrial Reorganisation Corporation Report and Accounts, 1969/70*, London, HMSO, 1970, app. 2.

[3] The Fafnir Bearing Company; this sale, as well as new entry, accounted for the 9·2 per cent decrease in concentration over the period 1958–63.

[4] That is, although the Census would register an increase in concentration, the merger was vertical in character.

into a British-owned concern which made about 35–40 per cent of United Kingdom output of bearings.[1] The major reason for promoting agglomeration was that the British concern could rationalise and thus contribute to an improvement in the balance of international trade in bearings. In addition: 'The economies of scale to be reaped from volume production were demonstrated to IRC in detailed breakdowns of various cost structures for different manufacturing units.'[2]

In summary, except for the most recent past, mergers have played only a minor role in concentrating this trade. Concentration appears to have been the result of the need to establish facilities in mass production plants, so that the earliest manufacturers of British origin were overshadowed by larger, foreign-owned entrants.[3] Small firms appear only in specialist sectors of the market.[4]

Telegraph and telephone installations; line apparatus

Until 1911 the United Kingdom imported most of its requirements of exchange equipment,[5] but in that year the monopoly of the National Telephone Company expired and the Post Office took over most of the internal telephone network. This event heralded a period of thirteen years or so during which British firms invested in plant to supply telecommunications equipment of a non-standard nature to the Post Office. Siemens produced their first equipment in 1913 and installed their first exchange at Grimsby in 1918. GEC first produced telephone apparatus in 1912 at the Peel Conner Telephone Works, Salford. The Automatic Telephone Manufacturing Company (subsequently Automatic Telephone and Electric) also opened plant in the 1910s. Before these new entrants, Western Electric, the major supplier to the United Kingdom market until 1911, had constructed a plant at Woolwich and production expanded there from 1885 onwards. Also, the Swedish firm L. M. Ericsson had formed a trading subsidiary in Britain by 1903 and production developed during the 1910s.[6] These five companies came to dominate the telecommunications industry.

---

[1] See Ministry of Technology, *IRC Report and Accounts, 1969/70.*   [2] Ibid. p. 42.

[3] Cf. *Financial Times*, 27 May 1970, p. 32, which notes that British manufacturers were mainly responsible for early patents in the technology of ball bearings, as opposed to roller bearings.

[4] British Manufactured Bearings in miniature bearings, Barden Corp. (UK) in precision miniature bearings, INA Bearing Company in needle bearings, the Torrington Company in needle and spherical roller bearings, and Cooper Roller Bearings in split cylindrical roller bearings.

[5] A. G. Whyte, *Forty Years of Electrical Progress*, London, Benn, 1930, p. 64; *The Story of S.T.C.*, *1883–1958*, London, Standard Telephones and Cables, 1960, p. 8; J. D. Scott, *Siemens Brothers 1858–1958: an essay in the history of an industry*, London, Weidenfeld and Nicholson, 1958, p. 169. The 'one supplier' referred to by Scott was Western Electric of Chicago, but Bell Telephone Manufacturing with a plant in Antwerp and L. M. Ericsson of Sweden also supplied.

[6] But the later named Ericsson Telephones was eventually independent of the Swedish concern. The Swedish parent company sold its control of the British concern in 1948 (*Guardian* 3 July 1972, p. 16).

With the advent of automatic exchanges after the 1914–18 war, the Post Office took the opportunity to standardise equipment, and Scott notes that four companies were primarily interested in the course that technology would take – Siemens, GEC, Western Electric and Automatic Telephone Manufacturing.[1] In the event, this last company approached the Post Office with a version of the Strowger exchange principle (invented in 1891) developed by a Chicago-based company, the Automatic Electric Company. This exchange version was adopted and became the basic output of British manufacturers who were party to the Bulk Supply Agreement with the Post Office. This Agreement, formulated in 1924, reserved manufacture of Post Office telecommunications requirements to a few firms (Ericsson joined the four others mentioned in 1928). The system was maintained for exchange equipment until 1969, and for line apparatus until 1964, when competitive tendering was gradually introduced.[2] Thus, oligopoly in these trades dates from the early 1920s when the structure was virtually frozen. New companies could enter the field only by merging with the existing manufacturers,[3] or by supplying to non-Post Office customers.[4]

Line apparatus came under a similar agreement, but here Standard Telephones and Cables (STC) had an almost unassailable lead over its rivals by its ability to exploit (or acquire exclusive British rights in) new inventions. The British rights to Pupin's work on 'loading coil' inductance were acquired in the early 1900s, and Western Electric developed Lee de Forest's work on repeatered audio transmission in both the British and American operations. STC introduced the first microwave link in 1931 as the forerunner of the Post Office's present extensive microwave network. They followed this in 1934 with the supply of the first twelve-channel carrier-on-cable system for long distance transmission, which led to the high-capacity system of coaxial cables, of which they were the sole manufacturers until 1950. During the 1939–45 war, STC were heavily committed to meet Ministry of Defence requirements and, in order to spread the load, they shared their technology with other firms.[5] Competitive tendering for Post Office business came in 1964, and the four firms

---

[1] Scott, *Siemens Brothers*, p. 172.

[2] *Economist*, 14 January 1967, p. 152; House of Commons, *First Report of the Select Committee on Nationalised Industries, Session 1966–67. The Post Office*, vol. 1, HC 304, London, HMSO, 1967, chap. 14, para. 36. The system was rather more open than this implies; for example, after 1955 10 to 20 per cent of exchange business could be tendered for by any manufacturer.

[3] Western Electric's British operation became STC when it was acquired by the American concern, International Telephone and Telegraph in 1925; Automatic Telephone Manufacturing became Automatic Telephone and Electric when acquired by the International Automatic Telephone Company in 1936.

[4] This was the market supplied by, for example, the Telephone Manufacturing Company first registered in 1929.

[5] *The Story of S.T.C.*, pp. 39 and 59.

STC, GEC, Telephone Manufacturing Company (acquired by Pye in 1960) and Siemens (acquired by AEI in 1954) were then the only major firms in this sector. English Electric were later to develop pulse code modulation equipment.[1]

The role of access to innovation in producing a highly concentrated industry was also apparent in the exchange sector. Siemens benefited from the research of Siemens and Halske, the German concern which had acquired the Strowger patent rights in Germany,[2] while Western Electric–STC acquired certain Strowger rights for the United Kingdom in 1920.[3] Automatic Telephone and Electric's access to American research has already been mentioned.

Only during the 1960s have mergers played a significant role in increasing concentration in telecommunications.[4] Plessey merged with Automatic Telephone and Electric, and Ericsson Telephones in 1961, while the GEC–AEI–English Electric combine was formed in 1967–8. These mergers had the effect of reducing the number of major firms in the exchange sector to three; but, with Plessey expanding in the field at this time, the number of major firms in line apparatus remained at four.

In summary, Post Office intervention and technological leadership combined to create high concentration through internal growth in these two trades. More recently, mergers have further reduced the number of independent competitors.

Cars

The history of the motor industry (MLH 381) from 1901, when the attempt to monopolise through patent purchases collapsed, to 1929, when the top five firms were responsible for about 82 per cent of the total output, was one of successive new entries, elimination through failure or bankruptcy, and finally the emergence of large firms which had seized the advantages of large-scale production. Between 1922 and 1929, the number of producers fell from eighty-eight to thirty-one: 'This concentration of production was brought about by internal expansion and the competitive elimination of other firms – not by mergers.'[5] By 1938 the largest six companies 'accounted for over 90 per cent of the market'.[6] All of these had achieved their position through internal expansion rather than by

---

[1] This firm had barred itself from the telecommunications industry under an agreement it made with Siemens in 1919 not to encroach on each other's product territory for twenty-five years (R. Jones and O. Marriott, *GEC/AEI. The anatomy of a merger*, London, Cape, 1970, p. 130). However, STC were, by many years, the initial suppliers of pulse code modulation equipment to the Post Office.

[2] Scott, *Siemens Brothers*, pp. 170ff.   [3] *The Story of S.T.C.*, p. 23.

[4] See Hart, Utton and Walshe, *Mergers and Concentration in British Industry*, pp. 107–13.

[5] G. Maxcy, 'The motor industry' in P. L. Cook and R. Cohen (eds.) *The Effects of Mergers*, London, Allen and Unwin, 1958, p. 367.

[6] Ibid. p. 373.

mergers. Since 1945 mergers of different kinds have played a major part in the vertical and horizontal restructuring of the industry. An account of events after 1945 is given in the companion paper to this book.[1] The post-1945 mergers in the trade merely consolidated high concentration.

There is now little scope for further concentration within the United Kingdom industry except by a merger between two or more of the 'big four' – British Leyland, Ford, Chrysler (United Kingdom) and Vauxhall. Since three of the companies are now owned by the three largest motor firms in competition in the United States, mergers are unlikely. Maxcy's judgement on the emergence of high concentration in this industry is still broadly apposite.

Wheeled tractors

Production of wheeled tractors (MLH 381) was in the hands of a few small firms in the first quarter of the present century. High concentration in the trade dates from the 1930s. In 1933 Ford commenced production at Dagenham, 'and the Fordson tractor quickly became popular with the British farmer, until in 1939 three-quarters of the tractors in use in British agriculture were Fordsons'.[2] During the war other tractor manufacturers were diverted to military production, and between 1940 and 1944 Ford made over 120,000 of the 128,000 tractors produced in the United Kingdom.

But in the postwar period a massive expansion in manufacturing facilities diluted Ford's dominance. In 1946 Ford produced about four fifths of British output, but by the mid-1960s Ford and Massey-Ferguson between them produced only about two thirds, and the latter had slightly the larger share. The most important of the new entrants after the war was the Standard Motor Company, which set up at Coventry in 1945, building on contract to the designs of Mr H. Ferguson. The rights in this agreement were acquired in 1953 by Massey-Harris (the small subsidiary of a Canadian firm with plant at Kilmarnock), while the actual production operation of Standard Motor at Coventry was not acquired until 1959.[3] A number of American concerns entered the trade after the war: International Harvester started wheeled tractor production in 1949 and envisaged a production of 3500 tractors per annum; Allis-Chalmers Manufacturing arrived somewhat earlier and were producing about a thousand tractors a year by 1949. Three British-owned firms were also in production by 1950: David Brown Tractors reached an annual output of 3500

---

[1] Hart, Utton and Walshe, *Mergers and Concentration in British Industry*, pp. 68–71.

[2] *Agricultural Machinery*, p. 11. The small scale of the industry pre-Ford may be gauged from the fact that over the period 1933–9 Dagenham produced 70,000 tractors ('Anatomy of a revolution', *Farm*, September–October 1967).

[3] So that for the purposes of the Census of Production, a merger of manufacturing capacity took place in the period 1958–63, and this may explain the concentration increase of just over 2 percentage points.

tractors in 1947; Marshall Sons 'manufacture a wheeled tractor at the rate of about 2500 a year';[1] and Morris Motors, after early trials, were producing tractors in 1948–9. Six other British concerns were also active at this time or soon after, notably the two car companies, Rover and Singer Motors.[2]

But these concerns were not on the same scale as Ford and Standard; in the latter, output had reached 5500 a month by August 1948, while in the former, 50,000 wheeled, half-track and crawler tractors were produced in 1948.[3] Since that time several enterprises have left the industry. Marshall Sons are no longer in the wheeled sector although they still produce crawler tractors.[4] Five companies dominate the trade, with Ford and Massey-Ferguson having a joint share in output variously estimated at between 65 per cent and 80 per cent.[5] David Brown and International Harvester are next in importance, while British Leyland (including Morris Motors) produced 8 per cent of total United Kingdom output in 1965–6.

In summary, mergers have played a minor role in promoting oligopoly in this trade.[6] In fact, since Ford dominated in the immediate pre-war and war years concentration has declined as the result of new entry, but it has remained high because only where the scale of entry has been large have firms succeeded.

Rubber tyres and tubes

Evely and Little concluded that the large scale of operations, which Dunlop and later foreign-owned entrants to the trade achieved, inaugurated high concentration in this sector (MLH 491).[7]

Although the production of pneumatic tyres began before 1900, the first large-scale expansion came in the 1920s, following the growth in production of cars and commercial vehicles. In the early 1920s Dunlop was dominant, 'the only large-scale manufacturer'.[8] During the 1920s

---

[1] *Agricultural Machinery*, p. 12.

[2] *Directory of Wheel and Track-Type Tractors produced throughout the World, 1955*, pp. 1–13.

[3] *Farm*, September–October 1967. Very few of these were crawler tractors.

[4] Among other post-war entrants, which have since discontinued production, are Minneapolis Moline (England), Singer Motors, and J. Brockhouse.

[5] See 'Mechanising the world's farmers', *Statist*, 9 December 1966, p. 1423; *Economist*, 5 June 1965, p. 1187 and 5 February 1966, p. 535; A. Lumsden, 'Massey-Ferguson's billion dollar battle', *Management Today*, October 1968, pp. 66–73 and 146.

[6] For example, Massey-Harris sold less than 100 tractors in the home market in 1953, while Ferguson sold roughly 17,000. Massey-Harris was a more important competitor in overseas markets (see *Financial Times*, 6 October 1972, p. 31).

[7] *Concentration in British Industry*, p. 125.

[8] Monopolies and Restrictive Practices Commission, *Report on the Supply and Export of Pneumatic Tyres*, HC 133, London, HMSO, 1955, para. 378. Other firms manufacturing in the early 1920s in the UK included Avon Rubber (established 1890); Henley's Tyre and Rubber (established 1918); British Goodrich Rubber (established 1924); Leicester Rubber (established 1906; eventually renamed John Bull Rubber); and North British Rubber (established 1870).

imports provoked fierce competition and price cutting, and, when tariffs were imposed in 1927, foreign companies established plant in the United Kingdom.[1] The Tyre Manufacturers Conference was formed in 1929 in order to combat excess capacity by regulating distribution and eliminating price cutting.[2]

Merger activity on the part of British firms was most important in the case of Dunlop. Dunlop purchased a majority interest in India Tyres in 1933, and was the sole owner by 1936. British Tyre and Rubber (the old British Goodrich Rubber) acquired Palmer Tyre and Stepney Tyre and Rubber in 1933. Although concentration increased slightly, mergers were not seen as the primary method of softening the effects of excess capacity. The Conference reduced price competition as far as it was able,[3] but did not always secure the desired conditions of trading. Some tyre manufacturers sought vertical integration to obtain market power.[4] Dunlop integrated backward into rubber plantations and cotton mills, and held important patents for the manufacture of wheels and rims. It also established a distributive network by covertly acquiring some twenty-seven tyre distributors up to the time that the Monopolies Commission sat.[5]

For a short period after 1945 the demand for tyres expanded rapidly, but growth had slackened off by the mid-1950s. British Tyre and Rubber ceased manufacturing tyres in 1956, so that its 1933 acquisitions did not give it lasting market power. Following the Monopolies Commission's recommendations, which declared that certain of the Conference's activities were against the public interest,[6] the emphasis changed to horizontal rather than vertical mergers. In 1957 Avon Rubber took over Henley's Tyre and Rubber, and Dunlop acquired John Bull Rubber in 1958. In the late 1950s, the introduction of the radial tyre by Michelin (soon produced by Pirelli also) left Dunlop behind, and with some expensive re-equipping to do.[7] A lengthy strike in 1970 threatened Dunlop's dominant position still further, because up to that time British car manufacturers had tended to buy British and now resolved to reduce their dependence. In 1971 Dunlop merged with Pirelli.

[1] For example, India Tyres, Goodyear Tyre and Rubber, Firestone Tyre and Rubber, Michelin Tyre, and Pirelli set up plant during the years 1927–9.

[2] Apart from those mentioned above, other members manufacturing on a small scale were Englebert Tyres, Fisk Tyres, Etablissements Hutchinson, St Helens Cable and Rubber, and Seiberling Tyres; but by 1932 these had discontinued tyre manufacture (ibid. para. 54).

[3] Ibid. para. 556.

[4] Donnithorne, *British Rubber Manufacturing*, p. 51.

[5] Monopolies and Restrictive Practices Commission, *Report on the Supply and Export of Pneumatic Tyres*, paras. 414–17 and app. 22.

[6] Ibid. para. 556.

[7] R. Heller, 'Where Dunlop is driving', *Management Today*, May 1969, p. 64: 'Dunlop plunged into a conversion whose cost was essential for defensive reasons alone. Although its market share has changed little, at around 40 per cent in the UK, that share would have dropped catastrophically . . . without the radial.'

In 1951, the top six manufacturers shared about 87 per cent of sales,[1] while mergers in the later 1950s increased the share of the top five to 93·2 per cent in 1958. By 1970 the concentration level was perhaps 1 or 2 points lower.

In summary, internal growth, the large initial size of concerns, and the activities of the Tyre Manufacturers' Conference, promoted high concentration in this trade as Evely and Little concluded. However, in terms of a longer run perspective than Evely and Little were able to command, it is quite clear that Dunlop has sought mergers as a means of retaining its leadership in the market, either horizontally (as with India Tyres, John Bull Rubber and Pirelli), or vertically.

SUMMARY OF FINDINGS

Table 3.8 summarises the major findings of the present chapter. From column (i) it can be seen that, for eight of the twenty-four products surveyed here, external expansion of the leading firms has been the route to high concentration. Columns (ii) to (v) summarise the story in the remaining sixteen products, where either internal growth or few new entrants, or a combination of the two, explain high concentration.

These findings require some qualification. Most important, a judgement has been made on the basis of predominant tendencies in order to classify a product in either the external-growth or the internal-growth groups. Dyestuffs, where ICI dominates, is the only case where some balance of doubt remains; we came to the conclusion that on balance it has been a merger-intensive trade, but an extended account has been given of the circumstances so that readers may judge for themselves.

Columns (i), (ii) and (iii) show that mergers have played some role in eighteen of the twenty-four products; in three of these, mergers have merely increased concentration in what were already highly concentrated products (fish oils, telephone installations and cars), and in four others mergers counteracted tendencies for concentration to decrease from a high level (frozen fish and vegetables, ice cream, rubber tyres). The three products in column (iii) (condensed milk, soups and coffee) experienced minor merger activity; these acquisitions were interesting exceptions in otherwise mergerless histories.

The conclusion to be drawn from this sample of products is that in a majority of them (two thirds) monopoly, near-monopoly or tight oligopoly

---

[1] Dunlop with 47 per cent, and Goodyear, Firestone, Michelin and Avon with 40 per cent between them (Monopolies and Restrictive Practices Commission, *Report on the Supply and Export of Pneumatic Tyres*, paras. 386 and 477). Consequently, in 1951 John Bull Rubber, which Dunlop acquired in 1958, had a rather minor market share; similarly, Henley's Tyre and Rubber must have had a small market share before being acquired by Avon Rubber in 1957.

Table 3.8. *Paths by which high concentration emerged in products with 90 per cent concentration or more in 1958*

	External expansion (merger-intensive) (i)	High concentration maintained by mergers (ii)	Minor contribution by mergers (iii)	Internal growth (iv)	Few entrants (v)
Blended whisky	×	.	.	.	.
Dyestuffs	×	.	.	×	.
Steel sheet	×	.	.	.	.
Tin and tin alloys	×	.	.	.	.
Gramophone records	×	.	.	.	.
Safety glass	×	.	.	.	×
Asbestos cement goods	×	.	.	.	×
Wallpaper	×	.	.	.	.
Frozen fish	.	×	.	×	.
Frozen vegetables	.	×	.	×	.
Condensed and evaporated milk	.	.	×	×	.
Ice cream	.	×	.	×	.
Soups	.	.	×	×	.
Coffee extracts and essences	.	.	×	×	.
Synthetic rubber	.	.	.	×	×
Fish and marine animal oils	.	×	.	×	×
Detergents	.	.	.	×	.
Crawler tractors	.	.	.	×	×
Ball and roller bearings	.	.	.	×	.
Telegraph and telephone installations	.	×	.	.	×
Line apparatus	.	.	.	.	×
Cars	.	×	.	×	.
Wheeled tractors	.	.	.	.	×
Rubber tyres and tubes	.	×	.	.	×

market structures have arisen without recourse to acquisition or to mergers with others of equal size, but merely through the internal growth of the leading companies. Mergers have been primarily responsible for producing high concentration in a third of the product markets. As we shall see below, this interim finding of the greater importance of internal growth is not substantially affected by a survey of the additional eight products in chapter 4; a re-examination of these findings in comparison with those in chapter 2 based on Evely and Little's sample is deferred to the end of chapter 4.

MONOPOLY AND NEAR-MONOPOLY IN EIGHT NON-DISCLOSURE PRODUCTS

INTRODUCTION

The reason why a separate chapter has been devoted to these products is not merely the disclosure rules in the Census of Production; the trades concerned merit special attention because their concentration ratios are exceptionally high – so high that the values could not be published without breaching the rule on confidentiality. In spite of the absence of official concentration ratios, it is possible to obtain reliable estimates of the level of concentration in most of these product markets from non-census, but official, sources. Since these products are made under conditions of monopoly or very near-monopoly, to have excluded them from the study would have resulted in an unacceptable degree of bias in the general results.

THE NON-DISCLOSURE RULES

The 1963 Census of Production published 277 concentration ratios for 1963, but the individual industry reports contained sales information on many more products. Thus, the Census provided a sample of ratios and the selection rules used to determine this sample have been described elsewhere.[1]

But one set of ratios was excluded by law. The Statistics of Trade Act, 1947, states in various of its clauses:

No individual estimates or returns, and no information relating to an individual undertaking, obtained under the foregoing provisions of this Act, shall, without the previous consent in writing of the person carrying on the undertaking which is the subject of the estimates, returns or information, be disclosed . . . in compiling any such report, summary or communication the competent authority, shall so arrange it as to prevent any particulars published therein from being identified as being particulars relating to any individual person or undertaking . . . no such report, summary or communication shall disclose the number of returns received with respect to the production of any article if that number is less than five; . . .[2]

However, the total quantity or value of any articles produced, sold or delivered may be published after any representations made by any person directly affected by the disclosure are considered.

[1] See Hart, Utton and Walshe, *Mergers and Concentration in British Industry*, pp. 23–9.
[2] Sections 9 (1), 9 (5) (a) and (b).

Thus the census office spent a considerable amount of time suppressing information which would have disclosed the operations of individual firms.[1] The 'five-firm' rule was derived from the recommendations of the Nelson Committee,[2] which made out the obvious case for three to be the minimum number of returns reported against a value figure, but noted that disclosure could arise '. . . even in this case, if two of the three firms are under a single control'.[3] This consideration seems to have led to supposing that 'An additional safeguard against the isolation of cases where disclosure is involved would be to show the number of entries against a product, i.e. the number of establishments at which the product is made, only if the number is five or more.'[4] Clearly then, this rule for establishments, firms, or entries has been carried over into concentration tables for enterprises (enterprises being aggregations of firms). Thus, while the census office seems to have interpreted the 1947 Act very conservatively, it has suggested the following justification: 'Disclosure occurs if there are entries against those items [net output and employment] for less than three enterprises (the establishment details being accumulated to an enterprise basis for assessment). *It may occur when three or more enterprises are concerned, if one or two of them held a dominant position in respect of the item under consideration.*'[5]

It is possible to assemble a list of products for which concentration ratios were probably worked out, but which were, in the final event, not published because of the possibility of disclosure. For example, in the spirit distilling and compounding industry (MLH 239),[6] there are four products for which concentration ratios could have been assembled. For two of these, ethyl alcohol and blended whisky, concentration ratios were in fact compiled and published. In 1963, another, gin, had sales of over £51 million and the fourth had sales of just over £5 million.[7] Gin sales were reported in the form:

	Quantity	Value	Enterprises
	Th.proof gall.	£000	
Duty paid	3,630	48,013	6
Duty free	2,040	2,991	*

[1] See M. C. Fessey and H. E. Browning, 'Confidentiality of business statistics', *Statistical News*, no. 10, August 1970, pp. 1–6. The authors estimate that exercises to discover and suppress cases of disclosure constituted about one tenth of the cost of the 1963 Census of Production.

[2] Board of Trade, *Report of the Census of Production Committee*, Cmd 6687, London, HMSO, 1945, after para. 63.   [3] Ibid. para. 56.   [4] Ibid. para. 57.

[5] Fessey and Browning, 'Confidentiality of business statistics', p. 4 (italics added).

[6] Census of Production 1963, part 19.

[7] 'Other descriptions of rectified or compounded spirits and other British compounds for use as beverages', sales of which were thus below the £10 million threshold used by the census office to exclude products with insignificantly small sales from the concentration table.

The asterisk indicates that the number of firms was not revealed because of the risk of disclosing information about individual enterprises. In contrast there was no risk in revealing that there were six firms producing gin for the home market, but in this case publication of a five-firm concentration ratio would have risked disclosure of the sales of the sixth firm by subtraction. A search through the industry reports shows that at least seven other trades were similar to gin: tinplate (MLH 311), plaster products (MLH 469), cigars (MLH 240), manufactured fuels (MLH 261), data processing equipment (MLH 338), precious metals refining (MLH 396) and flat glass (MLH 463). These eight trades are discussed separately below.

To counteract the absence of official concentration ratios, more space is devoted to each of these case studies than that given to the typical product surveyed in chapter 3. The eight products are illustrations of monopolies, duopolies and triopolies which could easily have been overlooked if attention had been confined to those products with concentration ratios published in the Census. They contain examples of consumers' and producers' goods, of trades which are expanding and trades which are contracting, and of old and new products. Three products have been classified in the external-expansion group (gin, tinplate and plaster products), while the other five (cigars, manufactured fuels, data processing equipment, precious metals refining and flat glass) have been classed as expanding internally.

PRODUCTS WITH EXTERNALLY EXPANDING LEADING FIRMS

Gin

Gin (MLH 239) is made from a basic mash of corn or barley and juniper berries, with a variety of fruits and spices added. These ingredients are compounded to produce a vapour of alcohol which is condensed back into liquid form and bottled. According to Lord Kinross, 'stills need to be operated by stillmen of ripe experience and judgement. At Wandsworth the older hands can still judge, by the feel of the pipes, the strength and quality of the spirit as it flows down through the spiralling copper pipes of the Condenser.'[1] Lord Kinross does not reveal whether these judgements are subjected to empirical tests.

The Census shows that production by larger enterprises increased by 12·1 per cent between 1954 and 1958, but by only just over 2 per cent in the period 1958–63.[2] However, production expanded by almost 40 per

---

[1] *The Kindred Spirit: a history of gin and the house of Booth*, London, Newman Neame, 1959, pp. 74ff.

[2] Census of Production 1958, part 19, table 4 (ii); 1963, part 19, table 5.

cent in the period 1963–8 because of a dramatic growth of exports – duty free gin production increased by over 147 per cent, while duty paid production actually declined by over 21 per cent. Before the 1960s, growth of domestic consumption was attributed to the lack of Scotch whisky during the war and after, while gin is supposed to have appealed to the emancipated female purse. Domestic expansion after 1960 is said to have been checked by competition from odourless vodka, the increasingly popular dark and light rums, and finally brandy.

The major firms in the trade are the Distillers Company and James Burrough.[1] In addition there is a brewers' consortium – Squires Gin – in which Whitbread and Watney Mann have a substantial interest. This firm is 'supported by some 100 brewers'[2] and its main brand was launched in 1957. One source tells us:

The UK gin market is dominated by DCL which has the two leading brands, Gordons and Booths, which together account for approaching 90 per cent of the UK market. The next largest producer is the brewing consortium, which with Squires and Cornhill probably commands about 7 per cent of UK consumption. . . . Burrough's Beefeater is the export market leader, equalling the combined exports of DCL's brands – principal of which are Gordons, Tanqueray, and Booth's House of Lords.[3]

This picture of the structure of sales is roughly confirmed by another source which, one year later, gave Distillers a rather smaller share of the home market and Squires a somewhat larger one.[4] The Monopolies Commission stated:

The brewers' share of production of gin, the second most popular spirits drink in the United Kingdon, has shown a marked increase in recent years. Two Distillers' Company's brands (Gordons and Booths) together have about 60 per cent of the United Kingdom market; the next biggest share is held by Squires, a brewers' consortium gin, with about 20 per cent of the market. Squires gin was originally introduced in 1957 as a Whitbread house brand; in 1959 a small number of other brewery groups reached agreement with Whitbread to set up Squires Gin Limited, to produce and bottle a gin for sale in their tied houses, each member contributing an equal share towards the capital of the company. Most of the brewery companies in the United Kingdom are now members of the gin consortium.[5]

---

[1] Small firms include IDV; Schenley Industries (USA), with two British subsidiaries; J. and W. Nicholson; and Courage with its subsidiary London Gin Distillery. There are a number of very much smaller firms, some with less than twenty-five employees actually in gin production, for example, James Hawker, Grierson Oldham and Adams, and MacKinlay-McPherson, a subsidiary of Scottish and Newcastle Breweries.

[2] Economist Intelligence Unit, *Retail Business*, no. 123, May 1968, p. 22.

[3] 'Distillers, the industry and the DCL', Govett and Sons, 1967, p. 15 (a stockbrokers' report).

[4] Economist Intelligence Unit, *Retail Business*, no. 123, May 1968, table 11, p. 22.

[5] *Beer. A report on the supply of beer*, HC 216, London, HMSO, 1969, para. 66.

Table 4.1.   *Gin: production shares, 1963*

Percentages

Distillers	62–3
James Burrough	20–1
Squires	3–4
Others	12–15

SOURCES: Economist Intelligence Unit, *Retail Business*, no. 123, May 1968; 'Distillers, the industry and the DCL'; Monopolies Commission, *Beer*.

These sources suggest that Distillers had a commanding lead in the home market up to the late 1950s. Burrough's Beefeater was and still is its equal in export markets. Since 1959 the brewers' consortium has promoted its own brands (Squires and Cornhill) and these have captured an increasing share of the home market. This has been achieved with the aid of a system of financial incentives.[1]

The 1963 shares of total production are estimated in table 4.1. Since 1963 the brewers' consortium has increased its share to 9–10 per cent, while Burrough's share has increased by 1 or 2 percentage points. At the same time Distillers' share has declined to between 50 and 55 per cent.

Distillers entered the gin trade in 1884, with the acquisition of the Caledonian Whisky Distillery with premises at Tooley Street, London. Subsequent acquisitions were J. and J. Vickers of Fulham (a subsidiary of the Bristol Whisky Distillery) and Tanqueray Gordon (a subsidiary of a larger whisky firm) in 1922; Sutton Carden, Boord and Son, and Sir Robert Burnett all in 1924. The latter three acquisitions were part of a defensive operation which started in the hope of 'amalgamating the whole of the English gin business into one organisation . . . the trade was in a bad way with the 1918–20 increases in duty and the recession at home . . .'.[2] It was Distillers' acquisition of Tanqueray Gordon which prompted Booths Distilleries to acquire John Watney (of Wandsworth) in 1923. The Chairman of Booths said in 1928: 'I would remind you that the Wandsworth distillery was purchased primarily for the purpose of insuring us against our being cornered at any time for our very large supplies of distilled spirit, and at first showed certain losses . . .'.[3] Wilson takes this to mean that Booths feared the market dominance of Distillers would involve Booths too being taken over eventually. Booths went on to acquire other companies: 'In the fifteen years between the wars it took over twelve different companies engaged in the production and bottling of gin and of whisky.'[4] In 1937, when the Booths Chairman died, Distillers acquired a majority interest in Booths.

[1] Mainly discounts on the house brands – see Monopolies Commission, *Beer*, paras. 73–4 and app. 7.   [2] Wilson, *Scotch, the Formative Years*, p. 413.

[3] Quoted ibid. p. 428.   [4] Kinross, *The Kindred Spirit*, p. 86.

Thus high concentration in this industry dates from pre-war days,[1] and was the result of two firms following a policy of piecemeal acquisition until they in turn joined forces.

Tinplate

In their study of the tinplate industry (MLH 311) up to 1958, Evely and Little concluded: 'The emergence of the continuous strip mill. . . accelerated the process of amalgamation as the most painless way of accommodating the new and larger plants in an old and relatively inefficient industry.'[2] The facts of Evely and Little's study may be summarised as follows. A combination of stagnant demand and surplus capacity resulted from the United Kingdom's loss to the United States of the world lead in tinplate production. The United States was also the source of two innovations in tinplate production – the continuous strip mill and the electrolytic depositing of tin, which replaced a process of dipping the steel sheet into molten tin. The British industry, concentrated in South Wales, reacted to surplus capacity by setting production quotas and minimum prices in order to moderate the effects of competition. Thus, the introduction of new processes required the accumulation of capacity by acquisition. New strip mills and tinning plants, which eventually provided all of the industry's output, were erected at Ebbw Vale in 1938 (with the electrolytic tinning plant added in 1947–8), at Margam and Trostre by 1953 and at Velindre by 1956. Contemporaneously, concentration by mergers aided the retirement of old plant by the largest firms. By 1956–7 the SCOW could provide over two thirds of tinplate output, while RTB alone could have provided almost 40 per cent of British 1957 output. Older mills still survive by satisfying specialist requirements, but most were eliminated by 1958.

Lower production costs of the new processes were bound to bring about the concentration which occurred.[3] Very little change in the structure of the industry has occurred since Evely and Little wrote. Output between 1935 and 1951 had been virtually static, while it expanded by over 39 per cent in the years 1951–8, and by roughly a quarter again between 1958 and 1969.[4] Electrolytic tinning did not displace hot dipping as

[1] IDV acquired Gilbeys in 1962, but this hardly affected concentration at all because IDV had very little, if any, capacity in gin at the time.

[2] *Concentration in British Industry*, p. 240.

[3] The South Wales industry of before the war was 'built on a capital of about £5 million', while the Ebbw Vale works required an investment of £12 million (Evely and Little, *Concentration in British Industry*, p. 235). 'No actual figures are available, but these notional figures give some idea of the competitive cost of strip mill and pack mill operation of tinplate: pack mill – cost of 20 per cent highest-cost works, £36·5s.; strip mill – prime costs £25, capital charges £5·5s., total £30·5s.' (W. E. Minchinton, *The British Tinplate Industry: a history*, Oxford, Clarendon Press, 1957, p. 242.)

[4] Central Statistical Office, *Annual Abstract of Statistics*, London, HMSO.

Table 4.2.   *Tinplate capacity, 1955–65*

	1955		1960		1965[a]	
	(Tons 000)	(%)	(Tons 000)	(%)	(Tons 000)	(%)
First class, large-scale modern plant in a good location, mainly built in the last 15 years	590	*66*	988	*80*	1350	*96*
Older though efficient plant, likely to be useful for many years, and smaller-scale modern plant	—	—	222	*18*	55	*4*
Old plant, possibly capable of some years use in conditions of high demand, but otherwise of doubtful viability	300	*34*	25	*2*	5	—
Total capacity	890	*100*	1235	*100*	1410	*100*

SOURCE: Iron and Steel Board, *Development in the Iron and Steel Industry: special report*, HC 164, London, HMSO, 1961.

[a] Forecasts.

rapidly as the strip mill displaced the pack mill, but by 1966 only 11·8 per cent of tinplate was hot dipped.[1] The plant in use in 1965 would be almost universally modern according to a 1961 publication (see table 4.2).

In 1967 the British Steel Corporation acquired RTB and the SCOW, thus completing the financial concentration of the industry into one unit. In fact, private ownership of the two concerns occurred for only a limited period after the 1939–45 war. Steel nationalisation in 1951 was followed by the transfer of the tinplate interests from the Iron and Steel Corporation to the ISHRA in July 1953. The SCOW assets were offered to private holders as from March 1957, while RTB was still a subsidiary of the

Table 4.3.   *Tinplate and blackplate output of two major firms*

Thousand tons

	1963	1964	1965	1966
RTB	281	365	334	350
SCOW	853	768	832	765

SOURCE: Companies' Annual Reports and Accounts.

[1] 59·7 per cent in 1957 (*Metal Bulletin* (*tinplate special issue*), Spring 1967, p. 37).

ISHRA upon transfer to the British Steel Corporation in 1967. The relative sizes of the two amalgamated concerns is suggested by the outputs of tinplate given in their Annual Reports and Accounts before nationalisation. These are shown in table 4.3.

As a summary, the quotation from Evely and Little at the beginning of this section is still apposite.

Plaster products

This product group (MLH 469) includes all gypsum plaster products used as building materials, various types of plaster calcined from gypsum rock,[1] and plasterboard which is made 'by setting a core of wet plaster between two sheets of liner paper'.[2] Some 70 per cent of gypsum mined in Britain goes to produce plaster goods, while much of the remainder is used as a retarding agent in cement.

The Census of Production reveals that between 1954 and 1963 sales of plaster by large firms expanded more rapidly than sales of plasterboard. In terms of quantities, sales of plaster expanded by 66 per cent and of plasterboard by 48 per cent. But between 1958 and 1963 plasterboard overtook plaster, with a 37 per cent quantity increase in sales against 18 per cent, and this trend continued throughout the 1960s, reflecting the high cost of plasterers' labour and the increased requirements for plasterboard in industrialised building systems.[3]

The sole remaining firm in the industry was founded in 1917 as the British Plaster Board Company (now BPB Industries). Once the wallboard product became acceptable in itself, and as a substitute for initial layers of plaster, BPB's output expanded rapidly.[4] During the inter-war period BPB acquired gypsum mines, and it now controls a substantial proportion of British gypsum production. During the 1930s it also acquired most of the independent plaster manufacturers;[5] its competitors in plasterboard were Gyproc Products (a Distillers' subsidiary), Plaster Products (Greenhithe) and Bellrock Gypsum Industries. BPB acquired Gyproc in 1944, Plaster Products in 1955 and Bellrock Gypsum in 1967.

ICI was, until recently, also a competitor, using waste from the production of fertiliser as the core for its plasterboard. But 'the purity of this by-product gypsum became increasingly costly to control'[6] and ICI dis-

---

[1] The grades of plaster roughly correspond to the amount of water left after the kilning process (*Construction and Building Materials Review*, London, Gower Press, 1971, p. 151).

[2] National Board for Prices and Incomes, *Report No. 130. Plasterboard Prices*, Cmnd 4184, London, HMSO, 1969, para. 5.

[3] Between 1964 and 1970 plaster output actually declined by 11 per cent, while plasterboard output expanded by 26 per cent (Department of the Environment, *Monthly Bulletin of Construction Statistics*, London, HMSO); see also *Construction and Building Materials Review*, p. 152.

[4] Bowley, *Innovations in Building Materials*, pp. 330–43.

[5] J. Routley and H. Mattingley, *A Saga of British Industry: the story of the British Plaster Board Group*, London, British Plaster Board Group, 1959.   [6] NBPI, *Plasterboard Prices*, para. 10.

continued production in 1969. BPB now has a virtual monopoly of plasterboard and plaster production.[1] There can be little doubt as to the strategic importance of BPB's mining of gypsum in providing its monopoly position: '. . . we have already seen that control of production (of gypsum) has had, it seems morally certain, some influence on the structure of the plasterboard industry itself'.[2]

Distillers was dependent on BPB during the war when its Newfoundland supplies of gypsum ceased, while Plaster Products (Greenhithe) attributed its difficulties in part to the lack of its own source of raw material. At the last Annual General Meeting of the company, the Chairman reported that £7500 was to be spent on gypsum exploration.[3] It is significant that Bellrock Gypsum, the only major post-war entrant to the industry, had its own mine at Staunton in Nottinghamshire. Bowley considers that Bellrock was something of an innovator in that it helped to popularise the use of plaster panels as walling materials, whereas beforehand the main use of plasterboard was in ceiling construction.[4] These wall panels presented some competition to BPB for a while, but in fact they were a technical and economic failure and achieved little success.[5]

The dominance of BPB was all but complete in 1969, when the Prices and Incomes Board reported the plasterboard capacities shown in table 4.4. ICI had recently closed down another 10 million square yards capacity at Severnside. Thus, before the Severnside closure and Bellrock's acquisition, BPB had roughly 79 per cent of nominal industry capacity, ICI had 14 per cent and Bellrock 7 per cent.

For the future, as the Prices and Incomes Board argued,[6] BPB is likely to remain a monopolist because of four factors: there is insufficient growth in demand to attract new entrants; BPB and Associated Portland Cement have reserved many of the most promising gypsum deposits, and production using imported gypsum is uneconomic; high transport costs in relation to price exclude import competition; there are absolute cost advantages in terms of 'know-how'.[7]

---

[1] BPB and Associated Portland Cement mine most of British gypsum rock.

[2] Bowley, *Innovations in Building Materials*, p. 340; but see below, p. 73, fn. 1.

[3] Ibid. p. 337. Plaster Products had some 13 per cent of the plasterboard market in 1951.

[4] Ibid. p. 341. Bowley mentions some large firms as licensees: George Wimpey, Hills (West Bromwich), and Henry Boot and Sons of Sheffield, for example.

[5] Bellrock eventually approached BPB as a willing seller; after the owner died, his estate decided to sell. According to the NBPI, *Plasterboard Prices*, para. 9, the government did not consider the merger need be referred to the Monopolies Commission.   [6] Ibid. para. 12.

[7] Cf. J. S. Bain, *Barriers to New Competition: their character and consequences in manufacturing industries*, Cambridge (Mass.), Harvard University Press, 1956, pp. 152–3: '*Gypsum Products:* Industry sources indicate that know-how is extremely important in wall-board production and that established firms generally have various gadgets and technical improvements protected primarily by secrecy.' Bowley, *Innovations in Building Materials*, p. 337, states that Plaster Products (Greenhithe) was at times aided by BPB technology, patriotically loaned to achieve price stability in building materials in the post-war years.

Table 4.4. *Plasterboard: United Kingdom capacity, 1969*

Million square yards

BPB		
British Gypsum		
Cocklakes	(1 plant)	6
East Leake	(2 plants)	36
Erith	(1 plant)	18
Glasgow	(1 plant)	7
Kirby Thore	(2 plants)	36
Rochester	(1 plant)	12
Bellrock Gypsum		
Staunton	(1 plant)	10
ICI		
Billingham	(1 plant)	10
Total		135

SOURCE: NBPI, *Plasterboard Prices*, app. C.

In summary, this trade became highly concentrated primarily because of the acquisition policy of one firm; this policy has been aggressive or passive as circumstances dictated. The firm's dominance in the trade has been assured by its insulation from overseas competition, its absolute cost advantages and its assured supplies of raw material.[1]

PRODUCTS WITH INTERNALLY EXPANDING LEADING FIRMS

Cigars

Cigars (MLH 240) are defined by the Census to include 'whiffs' (nine ounces or less per hundred) and 'other' cigars. The 'other' category includes cigarillos, miniatures and panatellas as well as the rarer large sizes (for example, Corona and Club Corona). Cigar-making machines produce about twenty cigars a minute,[2] whereas Gallaher now use a traditional cigarette machine to produce a thousand whiff cigars a minute.[3] Their technological breakthrough was achieved by producing a binder sheet of 100 per cent tobacco which was strong and flexible enough to be handled by cigarette machinery.[4]

[1] Department of Scientific and Industrial Research, *Special Reports on the Mineral Resources of Great Britain*, vol. III: *Gypsum and Anhydrite*, by R. L. Sherlock and B. Smith, London, HMSO, 1938, showed that there were extensive gypsum deposits still left unworked which BPB had no claim upon.   [2] *Financial Times*, 9 October 1968.

[3] See *Statist*, 9 December 1966, p. 1431. For a description of the production process see A. E. Tanner, *Tobacco: from the ground to the smoker* (5th ed.), London, Pitman, 1951, p. 62; International Trade Centre, *The Major Markets for Unmanufactured Tobacco*, Geneva, UNCTAD/GATT, 1968, p. 242.

[4] Less than 100 per cent tobacco is disallowed by nineteenth century Customs and Excise regulations.

British production of cigars has expanded dramatically in the post-war period. In terms of physical weight, output expanded by 58·1 per cent over the period 1954–8, by 72·4 per cent over the period 1958–63, and by 87·7 per cent over the period 1963–8.[1] Imports have shared in the growth of British consumption; exports take less than 5 per cent of British production, while some 24 per cent of home market supplies were imported in 1968 and some 30 per cent in 1972.

Domestic production of cigars was dominated during the 1950s by two brands in the whiff market (Gallaher's 'Manikin' and Imperial Tobacco's 'Wills Whiffs') and one in the panatella sector (Imperial's 'Castella'). In the late 1950s both Gallaher and Imperial introduced miniature cigars which more nearly competed in price with cigarettes. Three developments formed cigar history in the 1960s. First, the two main manufacturers introduced new whiff brands which achieved popularity. Second, domestic producers forged links with overseas producers to import cigars.[2] Third, in 1966 and after various cigarillo launches were made, which at first captured some market ground from the miniature sector. Thus, the major developments in the late 1950s and 1960s were (apart from one or two cigarillo launches) instigated by the leading four tobacco firms – Imperial Tobacco, Gallaher, Carreras and British-American Tobacco. There were four (very much) smaller manufacturers still operating in 1970 – E. Alton, Abraham and Gluckstein, Justas van Maurik, and the CWS.[3]

The interest of importers below the top four is quantitatively small. Thus the figures in table 4.5 for manufacturers' shares of British production adequately reflect the competitive situation in the market, apart from the growth of British-American's imported share in the second half of the 1960s.

There have been some mergers in the history of this trade; they were important in establishing Gallaher as of comparable size to Imperial. In 1947 Gallaher acquired the Cardiff firm of J. R. Freeman and Sons; they made 'Manikin', a whiff which still held 18 per cent of the cigar market in 1969; in 1953 Gallaher acquired Richard Lloyd and Sons, makers of the 'San Toy' cheroot miniature, which had about 1 per cent of the cigar market in 1969. Since these acquisitions Gallaher has relied on internal

[1] Census of Production 1958, part 21, table 4; 1963, part 21, table 5; 1968, part 23, table 5.

[2] Carreras with Schimmelpenninck of the Netherlands in 1963, Gallaher with Ritmeester in 1965. Also Imperial currently controls a significant percentage of the imported cigar trade through its subsidiary Herbert Merchant. In 1966 British-American Tobacco acquired Henri Wintermans' brands, which now have perhaps 50 per cent of the imported cigar market, giving them just over 10 per cent of the market as a whole (see *Financial Times*, 9 February 1972).

[3] Apart from these manufacturing firms, Philip Morris Inc. has a small interest in imported cigars through its subsidiary, Melbourne Hart; Alfred Dunhill has its cigarillos made for it by a domestic firm, and there are a number of distributors who have their own brands made for them by firms here and overseas.

Table 4.5. *Cigars: British production shares by numbers of cigars, 1955-70*

Percentages

	1955	1960	1965	1968	1969	1970
Gallaher	50·5	46·0	40·5	45·0	49·0	47·5
Imperial Tobacco	38·0	51·5	57·5	54·0	50·0	51·0
Carreras	—	—	0·5	—	—	0·5
Others	11·5	2·5	1·5	1·0	1·0	1·0

SOURCE: trade estimates.

growth to increase its market share.[1] Imperial does not appear to have made specific cigar acquisitions;[2] its cigars are mainly produced by its subsidiaries, Churchmans, and W. D. and H. O. Wills, which are part of a defensive combine formed as early as 1901 to forestall the American invasion of the cigarette market.

A few small firms left the trade between 1955 and 1960. B. Morris ceased cigar manufacture in 1958, R. J. Elliott closed down in 1959, and the brands of Cohen Weenen, a subsidiary of Godfrey Phillips, were withdrawn when the home trade rights to all Godfrey Phillips' brands were acquired by an Imperial subsidiary in 1960. Effectively, three very small manufacturers were eliminated by the competitive process and by mergers. In addition, Marsuma amalgamated with Partridge and Sons in about 1960, but Marsuma–Partridge ceased production some time after 1963. Strangely, then, competition has been sufficiently intense on the part of the larger firms to eliminate smaller firms in a trade which has enjoyed very rapid growth.

The ability of large firms to dominate the market in this way has very little to do with the kind of 'unfair' trading practices complained of by smaller cigarette firms.[3] The factors making for the demise of small firms probably parallel those in the cigarette trade where, after the decontrol of tobacco imports, the more popular brands of the large firms gained ground. They were doubtless exacerbated by the size-economies of Gallaher and Imperial, including their ability to introduce new products in bulk (miniatures), advertising and marketing economies, and easier access to capital to invest in the latest cigar-making technology.

In summary, this trade, like the cigarette trade, had production shares

---

[1] Because J. R. Freeman was much the larger of the two concerns in cigar production when it was acquired by Gallaher, we may view the present Gallaher share as Freeman plus internal and external growth since 1947.

[2] Although it acquired the cigar importer, Herbert Merchant, in 1966. See also B. W. E. Alford, *W. D. and H. O. Wills, and the Development of the UK Tobacco Industry 1786–1965*, London, Methuen, 1973.　　[3] Monopolies Commission, *Report on the Supply of Cigarettes and Tobacco*, paras. 401–7.

virtually frozen by import controls until the mid-1950s.[1] Under these conditions, larger firms could only grow by acquisition (as did Gallaher). After the mid-1950s smaller firms gradually atrophied or, as in the case of Cohen Weenen, were eliminated by the external-growth policy of the larger firms. Smaller firms still flourish in the more specialised sectors of the market, or have survived because they have a link with outlets (for example, the CWS). But these do not offer effective competition to the leading firms, who control at least 80 per cent of imports.

Manufactured fuels

The products classed under MLH 261 in the Census do not constitute an exhaustive list of those which actually compete in the market. Principally they are solid smokeless fuels, non-smokeless fuels, and a number of by-products, such as coal tar fuels, from the production processes of the other two items. However, excluded from the definition is the output of the gas industry, which produces popular solid smokeless fuels (Cleanglow and Phimax). Production of these fuels, which are looked upon as part of the gas industry's coke output, is accounted for in the gas industry's report.[2] Also excluded are naturally smokeless fuels, such as anthracite and dry steam coal. Thus, to some extent, the high level of concentration in the sector is a fiction. On the other hand, inclusion of anthracite and dry steam coal would merely expand the output of a concern already in the sector – the National Coal Board (NCB) – while the exclusion of the gas industry means that only one other concern is omitted. In any case, the gas industry is now running down production of products competing in this sector, because successive technological revolutions in the industry are eliminating coal gasification.[3]

Quantity and sales information for the sector is contained in table 4.6. Solid smokeless fuels are mostly produced by three concerns: the NCB, with brands such as 'Phurnacite', 'Homefire', 'Multi-heat', 'Roomheat'; Coalite and Chemical Products with 'Coalite' brands; and the National Carbonising Company with the 'Rexco' brands. Their production overshadows the output of smaller firms such as British Benzol and Coal Distillation, and Barnsley District Coking. The output of these smaller firms may not enter into the sector, however, if their production is regarded as coke. This subtrade is expanding, while the output of non-smokeless, manufactured fuels is declining. These are mainly produced by the NCB, but other firms contribute minor outputs (for example, Powell Duffryn's 'Maxihet' and 'Maximet'). Finally, the output of 'other

[1] See Hart, Utton and Walshe, *Mergers and Concentration in British Industry*, pp. 77–80.

[2] Census of Production, 1963, part 127; 1968, part 152.

[3] Oil gasification and natural gas are the two major sources of gas (see *National Institute Economic Review*, no. 59, February 1972, p. 45, chart 6).

Table 4.6. *Manufactured fuels: output and sales of large firms,*
1963 and 1968

	Output		Sales	
	1963	1968	1963	1968
	(Tons 000)		(£ millions)	
Solid fuels				
Smokeless	1588	2991	14·9	31·9
Other	609	111	4·2	0·4
Other products	..	..	6·6	3·9

SOURCES: Census of Production 1963, part 22; 1968, part 24.

products' is also declining, which probably reflects the decrease in output of creosote-pitch mixtures.[1] The growth in smokeless fuels and the decline in non-smokeless are attributable to Clean Air legislation, which both restricted demand for non-smokeless briquettes and promoted the switch of resources into smokeless fuel production.[2]

The National Carbonising Company, and Coalite and Chemical Products use a low temperature process for carbonising coal. The inventions which led to the promotion of research into the feasibility of commercial production were made before the first world war, and production started in the interwar period. The access to new inventions, in which the two companies obtained the world rights, explains the high concentration in this sector. Coalite integrated vertically in 1926 by acquiring a retort maker (Gas and Fuel Plants), and diversified in 1962 when it acquired a maker of fuel oil additives (Duramis Fuels). Growth has been achieved by setting up new works under separate subsidiaries, until in 1970 the company had capacity of about 2 million tons per annum in four locations (Bolsover, Askern, Grimethorpe and Rossington).[3] National Carbonising followed a similar growth path until, in the 1960s, it integrated vertically into distribution. However, in the period 1969–71 it acquired three firms making solid smokeless fuels – South Yorkshire Chemical Works, Birchenwood Gas and Coke, and the Barnsley District Coking Company. Of these, only the last made a fuel classified in the sector ('Burnbrite'), while the other two were probably classified as coke producers. National Carbonising produced just over 0·6 million tons of

[1] The output of the 'general chemicals' industry has newly been included with by-products of the carbonisation sector in the 1968 Census of Production.

[2] For background see Ministry of Power, *Report of the Committee on Solid Smokeless Fuels*, Cmnd 999, London, HMSO, 1960; Ministry of Housing and Local Government, *Domestic Fuel Supplies and the Clean Air Policy*, Cmnd 2231, London, HMSO, 1963.

[3] 'The specialist chemicals industry', Laurie Milbank and Company, 1970, p. 22 (a stockbroker's report).

Rexco in 1970 in four locations (Comrie, Edwinstowe, Ollerton and Mansfield).[1] The NCB, from whom both its competitors acquire the raw material, has its major plant at Aberaman in Wales, making a brand of fuel suitable for use in closed appliances ('Phurnacite'). Since the early 1960s, however, it has tried to produce successful open fire fuels (Sunbrite, Roomheat, Multi-heat and Homefire), but technical difficulties have been encountered.[2] Total solid smokeless fuel production by the NCB in 1970 was over 1·1 million tons.

As suggested at the start of this section, it is only an approximation to state that there are three main competitors in the market. But, in so far as we agree with the approximation, market dominance was achieved by access to a technology which others did not share. The problem for new entrants into the sector is to achieve a standard of smokelessness which, as we have seen, was one of the problems faced by the NCB. Even if technical problems are overcome, it may still be difficult to break into a trade with a strong seasonal demand and to maintain national distribution. Economies of scale have not been important in promoting high concentration, although now the size of the leaders probably constitutes an entry barrier.[3]

Data processing equipment

The full definition of this product (MLH 338) is 'Data processing and handling equipment, *other than electronic*, including card punching machines and verifiers'.[4] This equipment, common in 'punched card systems', is basically of two kinds – machines for punching cards, and machines for interpreting, multiplying, collating, sorting and tabulating information punched on the cards. Sales expanded by 106 per cent between 1954 and 1958, and by 62 per cent between 1958 and 1963. However, sales declined by over 41 per cent between 1963 and 1968 as the use of electronic computers advanced.

Roughly the same firms who now specialise in electronic data processing equipment produced electro-mechanical equipment. The British Tabulating Machine Company and Powers-Samas Accounting Machines were joined after the 1939–45 war by International Business Machines (IBM), the American firm, with which British Tabulating operated a marketing agreement until 1949 (as did Powers-Samas with Remington Rand).

---

[1] Ibid. p. 54.

[2] See NCB Report and Accounts, various years. The problems have concerned standards of smokelessness and strength of briquettes.

[3] Both National Carbonising and Coalite developed continuous retort processes as opposed to the traditional batch processes of production (30 per cent of 'Rexco' is made by continuous retorts; National Carbonising had five continuous retorts out of forty-seven in 1969). In so far as large size enables the leaders to employ some capacity continuously and thereby produce fuels less expensively, this is a scale-economy.   [4] Census of Production, 1963, part 48, table 5.

Table 4.7. *Three firms' production of data processing equipment, 1953*

Nos. of models

	Hand punches	Automatic punches	Hand verifiers	Automatic verifiers
British Tabulating	8	7	4	1
IBM	2	3	—	2
Powers-Samas	6	5	6	9

SOURCE: *Creating the Punched Card*, app. E.

After the war the British government reached an agreement with IBM, whereby British Tabulating was allowed the free use of all existing patents and accumulated expertise, and IBM was allowed freedom to compete in British Commonwealth markets. This dollar-saving device meant an expansion for British Tabulating, since they could produce virtually all the equipment ancillary to hand punches, sorters and tabulators which had previously been imported from the United States. Employment expanded from roughly 3150 in the first post-war years to over 4450 in the years immediately after the agreement. Thus the Organization and Methods Division of the Treasury listed three suppliers of punched card systems, all based in London – British Tabulating, IBM and Powers-Samas – the first two of which used the Hollerith card as opposed to the Powers card.[1] Table 4.7 gives some impression of the range of card punches and verifiers produced by the three firms in the early 1950s.

Much of the critical history of this 'industry' is summed up in the following statement:

By 1957–58, both B.T.M. and Powers-Samas realised the need for rationalising their efforts both at home and abroad to compete with the very strong and growing competition from the United States. They were accordingly merged into a single firm, International Computers and Tabulators, early in 1959. The efforts of the new firm were directed increasingly towards the development and production of computers, and the production of punched card equipment was re-orientated accordingly. This has been the main reason for the fluctuations in output of punched card machines, which in future will be necessarily bound up with the development and production of ICT computers.[2]

[1] *Creating the Punched Card*, London, Treasury (Organization and Methods Division), 1953. It is also worth mentioning that British Tabulating and IBM equipment was electrically based, whereas Powers-Samas equipment was mechanical.

[2] S. Hays, M. F. W. Hemming and G. F. Ray, 'The office machinery industry in the United Kingdom', *National Institute Economic Review*, no. 49, August 1969, p. 57.

In addition, Powers-Samas may have sought the merger partly in order to wrest control of its affairs from Vickers, which had a majority share of its ordinary capital. But the major motives for the merger were doubtless the needs to regroup against IBM's competition and to pool research resources in an effort to dominate the domestic market in electronic computers. Thus the merger had very little to do with developments in the electro-mechanical trade.

The 1969 figures for shares of the British computer market are as follows for three of the participants: International Computers Holdings (previously International Computers and Tabulators) 41·0 per cent, IBM 23·4 per cent, National Cash Register–Elliott-Automation 10·7 per cent.[1] These are now the major firms in punched card machines and, when grossed up, the percentages suggest shares for all sales (electro-mechanical *and* electronic machines) of 55, 31 and 14 per cent respectively. However, National Cash Register does not produce electro-mechanical machines and, when allowance is made for International Computers' British employment, one is left with the impression that they probably had about two thirds of the market.[2]

Decline in the trade has been extremely rapid so that high concentration is only to be expected;[3] historically it was explained by the access to patents which two British firms acquired. A merger substantially increased concentration during the period 1958–63, but this was not directly connected with events in the sector.

Precious metals refining

The metals concerned here (gold, silver, platinum and platinum-family) may undergo different refining processes, may be refined to different standards of purity, and may be fabricated into a wide variety of final forms.[4] The trade as a whole (MLH 396) was expanding moderately over the period 1954–68, but this growth owed much to the increased business in platinum, which reflects the expansion in end-uses of the metal

---

[1] House of Commons, *Report of the Select Committee on Science and Technology. The UK computer industry*, HC 272, London, HMSO, 1970, app. II, p. 4.

[2] International Computers had 30,972 employees in the United Kingdom in 1968, while IBM employed 9,002. That is, the former had over three times as many employees as the latter, but only 1·75 times their share of the computer market. This suggests a greater proportion of non-computer products in the sales mixture, as well as implying that International Computers' output per employee in computers is low relative to that of IBM. Part of the latter difference may be attributable to the fact that less labour is required to distribute imported computers from the American parent than to produce computers in the United Kingdom.

[3] See, for example, International Computers and Tabulators' Annual Report and Accounts for 1963–4, which reported that £5·8 million worth of old tabulator equipment had to be written off. See also *Economist*, 26 September 1964, p. 1252.

[4] See A. Selwyn, *The Retail Jewellers Handbook and Merchandise Manual for Sales Personnel* (7th ed. revised J. J. Adler and G. F. Andrews), London, Heywood, 1962; *Services in the Refining of Gold, Silver and Platinum*, London, Johnson Matthey, 1951.

Table 4.8. *Precious metals: output and sales,[a] 1954–68*

	Output[b]			Sales			
	1954	1958	1963	1954	1958	1963	1968
	(Troy oz., 000s)			(£ thousands)			
Gold[c]	4,198	6,960	4,461	34,099	78,762	31,411	27,079
Platinum (and family)	718	679	1,178	16,730	12,049	26,926	76,194
Silver	39,071	39,826	32,613	12,192	13,814	13,287	35,497
Other	..	..	..	861	397	..	..
Total	..	..	..	63,881	105,021	..	..

SOURCE: Census of Production 1958, part 74; 1963, part 73; 1968, part 93 (1963 figures revised in 1968 Census).

[a] By firms with over 24 employees.
[b] Not recorded in the 1968 Census.
[c] Output measured in thousand troy fine ounces, slightly understated for 1958 and 1963.

– in oil refining, dentistry, scientific and electrical apparatus, and glass manufacture. Johnson Matthey has a silver refining plant with a capacity of 78 million ounces per annum, and a gold refining plant with a capacity of about 15–16 million ounces. It seems that plant scale-economies must explain the building of plants which are so large in relation to the annual outputs of table 4.8.

A special situation exists in platinum refining. About 70 per cent of the world supply is mined in South Africa and 75 per cent of the capacity there is worked by one firm – Rustenburg (the remainder is mined mainly by two others, Union Corporation and Atok). Rustenburg and Johnson Matthey jointly own a refining plant in South Africa, which refines most of the output into 'matte', and this is then brought to high purity by the Johnson Matthey plant in the United Kingdom. Another 15 per cent of platinum supplies in 1969 came from Canada, mainly as a by-product of International Nickel's nickel and copper output. The International Nickel Company refines some of its output at Clydach in Wales and some in Canada. The 'matte' residue from Clydach's nickel and copper extraction is sent to Acton (Middlesex) for extraction of metals in the platinum group. Engelhard Industries factors these metals for International Nickel and also receives 180 thousand ounces of Rustenburg output.[1] Much of the remaining 15 per cent of world platinum comes from the USSR, which has no fixed relationship with refiners.

[1] *Daily Telegraph*, 3 January 1972: '. . . the 180,000 ozs. of platinum (probably due to be cut to 150,000 ozs. soon) that Rustenburg tribute-mines for the Brakspuit consortium and sells to Engelhard . . .' Brakspuit is one of the four important South African platinum interests, but Rustenburg does all its mining.

There is a temptation to exaggerate the importance of mergers in this trade.[1] The Sheffield Smelting Company, which had just over 10 per cent of trade employment in 1958, acquired rival refiners Joseph Hoult Dixon in 1857, Charles Cooper of Birmingham in 1870, and E. W. Oakes in 1883 (Oakes had been an employee of Sheffield Smelting in 1865).[2] In the period from 1875 to 1931 the company was introducing and perfecting new refining methods (first for platinum by furnace recovery, then for silver by electrolysis). The 1931 rise in the price of gold brought a period of increased business; but this was followed by a recession, which was exacerbated by a decline in the silver trade. Parts of the firm of Blackmore Howard and Metherell were acquired in 1934 to extinguish debts, and Lees and Sanders of Birmingham was acquired in 1948.[3] Further acquisitions were made later outside precious metals refining. But in May 1972 it was announced that the proposed merger between Sheffield Smelting and Engelhard would not be referred to the Monopolies Commission and the merger was effected a few weeks later.

N. M. Rothschild and Sons acquired the premises of G. F. Mathison, the Bank of England's Mint refiner, in 1851. McDonald's version of the purchase indicates that a reorganisation of the Bank of England's refining requirements at that time made Mathison's plant redundant.[4] Johnson Matthey was offered the plant, but declined it, while Rothschild accepted the offer and became one of two official refiners to the Bank in 1852. The other official refiner at that time, Brown and Wingrove,[5] also sold its plant to Rothschild in 1890, having been forced out of business by the competition of the three younger refiners.[6] Over the long term, however, these acquisitions of redundant plant cannot have given Rothschild a leading share in the trade; the concern ceased refining late in 1967. Rothschild's plant and some of the labour force then found employment with Engelhard, and Engelhard's mark on gold bars became acceptable to the London market early in 1968. As already noted, Engelhard and Sheffield Smelting merged in 1972 to

---

[1] See A. C. Sturney, *The Mond Nickel Company*, London, privately published, 1951; R. E. Wilson, *Two Hundred Precious Metal Years*, London, Martins, 1964; D. McDonald, *A History of Platinum*, London, Johnson Matthey, 1960, *Percival Norton Johnson: the biography of a pioneer metallurgist*, London, Johnson Matthey, 1951, and *The Johnsons of Maiden Lane*, London, Martins, 1964.

[2] All the firms purchased were of negligible importance and/or refined little precious metal (Wilson, *Two Hundred Precious Metal Years*, pp. 115, 157–8 and 163–4).

[3] Ibid. pp. 231–2 and 252–3. Both these firms were built up partly by ex-employees of Sheffield Smelting.

[4] McDonald, *Percival Norton Johnson*, p. 135.

[5] Raphael's Refinery became the third official refiner in 1856; Johnson Matthey was admitted in 1861.

[6] Rothschild, Johnson Matthey and Raphael's (McDonald, *The Johnsons of Maiden Lane*, p. 134).

create a virtual refining duopoly, with Johnson Matthey as the other major firm in the market.[1]

Johnson Matthey have not been at any time conspicuously merger-active in this trade. The firm has integrated forward on occasion by acquiring firms using precious metals,[2] but the only refining acquisition was that of the Johnson and Son Smelting Works, which was purchased in 1925. This smelter had virtually ceased production as the result of a combination of circumstances.[3]

By 1970 Johnson Matthey had approximately 6000 employees in the United Kingdom and a turnover of £148 million; the comparable figures for Sheffield Smelting and Engelhard combined were 1900 employees and £29 million. Allowing for the fact that Johnson Matthey has diversified out of refining activities rather more than Sheffield Smelting and Engelhard, these figures nevertheless underline the fact that mergers have played a subsidiary role in promoting concentration in this trade.

High concentration has developed partly because of the limited access firms have had to refining technology. Sheffield Smelting, for example, eliminated the competition which its former employees had created by taking technical knowledge with them. The history of this company up to the 1914–18 war is an interesting case of internal growth externalised. Neither of the two partners controlling the firm wished to grow beyond a certain size and consequently employees left to start their own businesses. Many of these were then subsequently acquired.[4] Johnson Matthey's pre-eminence was founded on the reputation for assaying of Percival Norton Johnson and their subsequent ability to secure patents or British rights for the latest refining processes. For example, they acquired British rights in a number of platinum melting and refining processes from a succession of French inventors.[5] Johnson Matthey have also been fortunate in being able to reserve a large share of platinum refining for themselves. The Rustenburg connection has been described above; in the nineteenth century the firm came '. . . to an arrangement with the Russian Count Demidov, the owner of part of the principal source of platinum in those

---

[1] Raphael's Refinery closed down in the early 1920s (ibid. p. 159).

[2] For example, Blythe Colours, which was acquired in 1963, specialised in colours for the pottery and glass industries.

[3] Ibid. pp. 156ff. Supplies of gold from the Rand had dried up, as had supplies of jewellers' sweeps. The London Gold Market had ceased to exist. Johnsons had no plant which would allow them to diversify into silver refining and much earlier they had come to an agreement with Johnson Matthey not to enter platinum refining (ibid. p. 111). Johnson Matthey desired Johnson's plant site in Birmingham (Brimsdown) which was nearer London than its own, over-large, plant in Manchester.

[4] Wilson, *Two Hundred Precious Metal Years*, passim.

[5] McDonald, *Percival Norton Johnson*, pp. 175–6. This is not meant to belittle the home-bred improvements to refining processes introduced by George Matthey and members of the Cock family.

days, by which the firm became the sole agents for the sale of his platinum in London.'[1] If a younger firm looked like upsetting the status quo, the leading firms could apparently squeeze the newcomer out by their ability to regulate supplies of overseas materials for refining. For example, when the Johnson and Son Smelting Works made a success of a new gold refining process in the 1910s '. . . they worked the process with reasonable success until the large refiners decided that they must have a limit put on their activities and restricted them to £7000 of refining per week'.[2] The financing of stocks of gold constitutes another entry barrier to the trade. Electrolytic refining of gold bars is not an instantaneous process and firms must carry stocks of gold for those buyers wanting immediate delivery. Finally, as implied above, an entrepreneur wishing to start up as a refiner will not be accepted as such overnight. For obvious reasons the London market will need to be sure of a firm's credentials before its mark is acceptable.

In summary, mergers have played a subsidiary role in promoting near-monopoly in this trade. Of much more importance has been Johnson Matthey's technological lead over its rivals, and its ability to forge exclusive links with overseas suppliers of materials for refining. However, the recent merger between Sheffield Smelting and Engelhard has effected a significant tightening of the structure of this trade.

Flat glass

One major manufacturer, Pilkington Brothers, produces *all* the British output of raw, flat glass, but there are also a large number of glass processors, who treat either the edges or the surfaces of the raw glass in order to produce finished products. The first, second and fourth items in table 4.9, which are produced by Pilkington, constituted 82 per cent of trade sales in 1963 and 74·4 per cent in 1968. The Monopolies Commission estimated that Pilkington supplies about 91 per cent of British market requirements of unprocessed flat glass – the remainder being accounted for by imports.[3]

The major commentary on the development of this trade does not cover the processing sector,[4] which is dominated by a few firms.[5] In the manu-

---

[1] Ibid. p. 129.   [2] McDonald, *The Johnsons of Maiden Lane*, p. 156.

[3] Monopolies Commission, *Report on the Supply of Flat Glass*, para. 14.

[4] P. L. Cook, 'The flat-glass industry' in P. L. Cook and R. Cohen (eds.), *The Effects of Mergers*, London, Allen and Unwin, 1958. The processing sector includes the third, fifth and sixth items in table 4.9.

[5] These are Clark James and Eaton, with 1250 employees in 1970; John Hall and Sons (Bristol and London), 800 employees; Midland Glass (Holdings), 300–400 employees; S. Pearson, 300–400 employees; Aygee, 290 employees; and Bradford Glass, 280 employees. Other less important firms include Glass and Metal Holdings, Steeles (Contractors), RTZ-Pillar, T. and W. Ide, R. Seddon, British Challenge Glazing, E. Pickett, Alfred Arnold, and Wottons (Croydon). Many of these firms are primarily merchants who process glass as a sideline.

Table 4.9. *Flat glass: sales 1954–68*

£ thousands

	1954	1958	1963	1968
Rolled or figured glass			⎧ 7,006	9,265
Plate or sheet glass	21,607	26,484	⎨ 14,949	11,247
Processed[a] plate, sheet or other flat glass			⎩ 3,970	5,580
Float glass	[b]	[b]	7,494	17,523
Silvered plate, sheet etc.	—	—		
Shelves, fingerplates, etc.	3,234	2,865	2,472	4,800
Multiple glazed units	.. [c]	.. [c]	.. [c]	2,686
Total	24,841	29,348	35,891	51,100

SOURCES: Census of Production 1958, part 106, table 4; 1963, part 104, table 5; 1968 part 127, table 5.

[a] Other than silvered.
[b] Not produced.
[c] Not separately recorded.

facture of raw flat glass, the ability to achieve economies of scale has never significantly affected the structure of the trade.[1] Very substantial cost decreases have, on the other hand, been available to firms able to incorporate new techniques into the production process.[2]

It was the technical efficiency of Pilkington and Chance Brothers that allowed these two firms to survive into the present century as the only major firms in the unprocessed sector. Chance Brothers was eventually acquired by Pilkington in 1951, as the culmination of co-operation between the two firms over thirty years. For twenty years members of the Chance family were selling their shares to Pilkington. It appears that at any time after 1930 Pilkington could have eliminated competition by undercutting the prices of Chance's main product – rolled glass – but they chose not to, which is not surprising in view of their collaboration.[3]

Thus, Pilkington's acquisition of Chance, the only major merger in the history of the trade,[4] could be construed as a goodwill gesture. Chance could not go public and sell off the remaining family holdings in the market, because the firm was not sufficiently prosperous in the early 1930s. However, 'The alternative course was to sell to another manufacturer. This had to be either Pilkingtons or a foreign company. The firm was

[1] See Cook, 'The flat-glass industry', pp. 347–50.
[2] For example, the twin-grinding process introduced by Pilkington in the 1930s.
[3] In 'vita' glass, fibreglass, optical glasses, and rolled plate production in overseas plants.
[4] Although Chance itself had made some purchases of sheet glass producers in the mid-nineteenth century (Cook, 'The flat-glass industry', pp. 280–1), and had acquired the Glasgow Plate Glass Company in 1907–8, these purchases were of little importance in comparison with the effects of competitive atrophy.

probably of greater value to Pilkingtons than to any other firm, since a lively foreign competitor with international interests might well have reduced very considerably Pilkington's freedom of action.'[1] Pilkington had good reason to fear the intervention of a foreign firm, because imported goods largely dictated the prices of unprocessed flat glass. Import competition, especially from Belgium and France, and the setting up of new glass industries in countries which had previously imported British glass, rapidly eliminated window glass makers (before and during the American civil war) and plate glass makers (after the McKinley Tariff of 1891).[2] Since the late 1950s Pilkington has had less reason to fear foreign competition, because it developed (and holds world rights in) the float glass process, which produces a ribbon of glass by floating molten glass on molten tin.

In summary, mergers have been resorted to from time to time in this trade, either to eliminate actual competition (1855–65), or to forestall potential competition from foreign firms wishing to acquire a foothold in the United Kingdom.[3] But in terms of the capacity thus acquired, mergers have been a very minor source of increased concentration. Pilkington has managed to survive through innovation and superior management, while others have left the trade. Management skills included the ability to recognise when and how competition should be curtailed – by means of price agreements, quotas, market-sharing agreements, and so on. Thus mergers have rarely been necessary in the domestic context and could always be avoided in the international context by coming to some *ad hoc* agreement with rivals.[4]

SUMMARY OF FINDINGS

The findings of this chapter are summarised in table 4.10. Only one of these products, manufactured fuels, has no record of merger activity. From its beginnings there have been few firms in the trade, and entry barriers in the form of costs of technical knowledge and brand loyalty maintain high concentration. Mergers played only a subsidiary role in four other products. In cigars, where a virtual production (although not market) duopoly exists, one of the leading producers acquired two firms since 1945. In data processing equipment there was one important merger in 1959, which reduced a virtual triopoly to a virtual duopoly. In precious metals refining and in flat glass a number of mergers have occurred, but

---

[1] Ibid. p. 335.

[2] Cook also feels that atrophy up to 1855 was largely the result of technical incompetence on the part of small firms unable to keep up with innovation; 1855–65 was the only period when mergers were sought to limit competition (ibid. p. 288).

[3] Pilkington–Chance in 1951 and Pilkington's acquisition of Sheet Glass of Queensborough in 1932.   [4] Ibid. passim.

Table 4.10. *Paths by which high concentration emerged in eight non-disclosure products*

	External expansion (merger-intensive) (i)	High concentration maintained by mergers (ii)	Minor contribution by mergers (iii)	Internal growth (iv)	Few entrants (v)
Gin	×	.	.	.	.
Tinplate	×	.	.	.	.
Plaster products	×	.	.	.	×
Cigars	.	×	.	×	.
Manufactured fuels	.	.	.	×	×
Data processing equipment	.	×	.	×	×
Precious metals refining	.	×	.	×	×
Flat glass	.	.	×	×	.

their quantitative significance in promoting concentration has been minor. Thus, in five products either mergers played no part in promoting concentration, or they would have been highly concentrated even in the absence of the mergers which did take place. In all of them, as might be expected, there are significant barriers to entry.[1]

Of the three merger-intensive products, two are monopolies – tinplate and plaster products – and gin is a triopoly.[2] The gin trade became highly concentrated during the interwar period, as one firm started to acquire others during a recession. Later it purchased its main competitor which had previously shown signs of resisting its dominance of the trade. In tinplate, surplus capacity, the advent of new processes requiring larger scale, and political factors (steel nationalisation) were the major influences in a history of continuous merger activity stretching from about 1930 to the mid-1960s. In plaster products, one firm has acquired all its competitors at various times in the present century. In these three merger-intensive product-markets significant entry barriers exist.[3]

If we compare the findings of the previous chapter and the present chapter, our conclusion on the importance of mergers in promoting high concentration is much the same. Instead of mergers promoting high con-

[1] Firm (marketing) economies of scale in cigars, financial economies of scale in precious metals refining, and absolute cost and capital cost barriers in precious metals refining and the other trades.

[2] But for the recent emergence of a powerful new competitor, Squires, the gin market would be a duopoly.

[3] In tinplate, scale-economies prohibit new entrants; in plaster products, absolute cost advantages are enjoyed by the monopolist; in gin, marketing economies and the vertical integration of one of the three main producers constitute the entry barriers.

centration in one third of the products, the proportion in this chapter is
three out of eight. Whereas mergers played some role in the achievement
or retention of high concentration in fifteen out of twenty-four of the
markets discussed in chapter 3, six of the present eight products experienced some noteworthy merger activity at various points in their history.
If the present chapter is regarded as supplementing the surveys of the
previous chapter the results can be pooled. Overall, eleven out of the
thirty-two products surveyed may be characterised as merger-intensive.
In addition, there were ten products where mergers were sought to bolster
or reinforce a situation of market dominance initially built up by internal
growth. Thus, overall, there were twenty-one products where mergers
had been resorted to at some point during the process of concentration –
either as a *sine qua non* of that process, or when the internal growth of small
firms posed a threat to large firms which had themselves grown internally.

It is freely admitted that this classification of the data is not perfect,
but it seems the most reliable that can be made, given the available
sources of information. The major problem with the data has been in-
ability to measure the exact contributions of internal and of external
growth to the increased market shares obtained. It is possible that, if one
gave the case-study material to two readers and asked for a classification,
they might present different lists. But the contention here is that in the
majority of cases there is no doubt about the right classification; if there are
no mergers the trade cannot possibly be described as merger-intensive, but
if one producer systematically acquires virtually all his competitors it must
be so described. It is possible to draw up lists of borderline cases to see
whether they could make any difference to the main findings. The products about which there is most doubt are dyestuffs, safety glass, asbestos
cement goods, rubber tyres, cigars and precious metals refining.

In dyestuffs, one merger-intensive firm has roughly 50 per cent of the
market, while one other firm in the trade also expanded externally in
some measure. In safety glass, although one firm has, over time, acquired
most of its competitors, concentration could still have been high in the
absence of mergers because there have been few entrants to the trade. In
asbestos cement, the doubt concerns the precise importance of a major
merger which took place in the 1920s. These three products were classed
as merger-intensive when it could perhaps be argued that this misrepre-
sents the facts.

On the other hand, rubber tyres, cigars and precious metals refining are
three cases where a not insignificantly small number of mergers occurred;
and it is often tempting to conclude that notable merger activity could
have had but one consequence – a dramatic increase in market concentration.

If all these six cases were incorrectly classified, it would not have much effect on the main findings. Three have been classified as growing externally and three as growing internally. It is also possible, however, that only one set was wrongly classified and then, if the importance of mergers was systematically understated, fourteen products would fall in the external-growth category and eighteen in internal growth. Our estimates of the number of products in each classification may be stated as a range; there were between eight and fourteen external-growth products and between eighteen and twenty-four internal-growth products.

One further potential qualification must be dealt with. When products were allocated to the internal-expansion group, no credit was given to mergers in related product fields which contributed to the growth of the firm. Yet, it could be argued that a firm which has obtained dominance by mergers in, say, tinned peas, would have a headstart on other firms when the market in tinned asparagus tips started to develop. The lead could allow the firm to grow internally and obtain a major share of the market.

The view taken here is that the example of tinned peas and asparagus tips is misleading. However many casually observed instances are noted in support of the hypothesis – for example, there *may* be reasons to suppose that mergers in soap gave Unilever a headstart in detergents (although this does not explain the internal growth of Procter and Gamble in soap) – there is at least an equal number of examples worth citing to the contrary. For instance, the British Match Corporation does not produce cigarette lighters, tin smelters have not become aluminium smelters, and WPM has not built up a large share in the paint market. Again, the hypothesis might suggest that Massey-Ferguson and Ford, two firms which grew internally in wheeled tractors, should have dominated crawler tractor production, but they have not. The hypothesis also has to answer the challenge that, in some cases, new product fields have been exploited by previously merger-active firms when their contemporaries, with a similar history of merger activity in a related field, have not done so. When Unilever began supplying frozen fish and frozen vegetables, this firm was by no means the only one shaped by events to do so.

The grain of truth in the hypothesis is simply that merger-active firms tend to be large firms, and large firms will presumably have advantages in production know-how, marketing and finance over many of their smaller contemporaries who may also wish to enter a new field. This, however, allows that all large firms, whether size has been obtained by internal or external growth, are equally well placed to dominate new product developments.

Among the internal-expansion trades discussed here, there are a few cases where the hypothesis receives support. Imperial Tobacco and Gallaher in the cigar trade grew by mergers in the cigarette market. The

NCB in manufactured fuels is another strong case in point. On the other hand, internal-expansion firms have branched out into new products – Ford into wheeled tractors and Nestlé into instant coffee.

Unilever appears in no less than five of the internal-expansion trades (frozen fish, frozen vegetables, ice cream, fish and marine animal oils, and detergents). Unilever's mergers were mainly in soap and oilseed crushing, so that two related products (detergents and fish oils) may be highly concentrated because of previous merger activity. However, Unilever is the major firm in neither of these product markets; it competes with firms which have built up their dominant position through internal expansion without the benefit of mergers in related fields. There is thus very little support in our data (including those on the internally expanding products themselves) for the hypothesis that mergers in related fields can substantially explain the dominance of leading firms in internal-expansion trades.

In chapter 2 above it was shown that twenty-four of the thirty-six trades surveyed by Evely and Little might be considered externally expanding – that is, they were trades where market power had been promoted initially by acquisition and mergers. It would thus appear that there is some difference, though perhaps not a startling one, between the two sets of results considered. In the next chapter we shall discuss the sources of this discrepancy.

CHAPTER 5

THE BALANCE OF INTERNAL AND EXTERNAL EXPANSION

INTRODUCTION

Chapter 2 described how Evely and Little found that mergers were the most important means of growth of the leading firms in high-concentration trades. But chapters 3 and 4 show that, historically, the internal expansion of firms has been the dominant source of high concentration ratios. The findings of chapters 3 and 4 require to be reconciled with those of chapter 2. The two sets of findings do not conflict in the sense that different authors analysed identical data and reached opposite conclusions, for clearly different samples of products were discussed. The task of this chapter is to analyse why the different samples led to different results.

There is very little overlap between the thirty-six trades surveyed by Evely and Little and described in chapter 2,[1] and the thirty-two products surveyed in chapters 3 and 4. Only six trades are explicitly in both samples, namely asbestos cement goods, wallpaper, tin, rubber tyres and tubes, tinplate and ice cream. Of these six trades, four are external- and two are internal-growth trades. There are also three cases of partial overlaps – tobacco of the thirty-six trades, which includes cigars of the thirty-two products, spirit distilling, which includes blended whisky, and spirit rectifying, which includes gin.[2] Clearly, these overlaps do not explain the discrepancy, which must be attributed to the remaining trades.

DIFFERENCES BETWEEN THE SAMPLES

The sample taken by Evely and Little was a non-random sample of trades from the 1951 Census of Production. Each trade had a three-firm concentration ratio of 67 per cent or more in 1951, and for each trade the authors were able to estimate the change in concentration over the period 1935 to 1951. The 1958 sample described in chapters 3 and 4 above was taken from the 1963 Census of Production, and each product had a five-firm concentration ratio of 90 per cent or more in 1958. The two samples thus had quite different origins, and there are many possible reasons why they yielded different results; five are suggested here:

(1) Their industry-mixes may differ, and if the motives for mergers are

---

[1] These exclude precious metals refining and ball and roller bearings, although they appear among the fifty trades in table 2.1 and are of course among the thirty-two products.

[2] It is questionable, perhaps, whether one should treat spirit distilling and blended whisky as a case of overlap. However, precisely the same firms are concerned in both business histories.

more pressing in certain industries than in others, then different results will emerge.

(2) Possibly the trades of the 1951 Census cannot be treated as equivalent to the products of the 1963 Census. Horizontal mergers within the 1951 trades could be viewed as vertical or conglomerate mergers between product groups under the finer classification of the 1963 Census.

(3) The role of the State may have been different in the two samples.

(4) The leadership achieved by one or two firms with access to a new technology may explain why many products in the 1958 sample are characterised by internal growth. That is, among these products mergers did not occur because they were not required for high concentration to be achieved.

(5) The age of the 1951 trades may place many of them in a particular historical period when mergers were the fashionable route to market dominance, or when industrial reconstruction entailed many mergers and closure of capacity.

Each of these possibilities will be considered in turn.

Representation in industrial orders

Table 5.1 places the thirty-five trades of 1951 and the thirty-two products of 1958 in their respective industrial orders.[1]

Table 5.1. *The samples of high-concentration trades and products classified into industrial orders*

	Trades (1951)[a]	Products (1958)[b]
II Mining and quarrying	1	—
III Food, drink and tobacco	7	9
IV Chemicals and allied industries	5	5
V Metal manufacture	6	3
VI Engineering and electrical goods	3	6
VIII Vehicles	2	2
IX Metal goods n.e.s.	2	1
X Textiles	2	—
XIII Bricks, pottery, glass, cement, etc.	2	4
XV Paper, printing and publishing	1	1
XVI Other manufacturing industries	4	1
Total	35	32

[a] Evely and Little's sample of high-concentration trades (see p. 7 above), excluding oilseed crushing.

[b] The products listed in tables 3.8 and 4.10.

[1] Seed crushing and oil refining has been excluded from the 1951 trades because we could not allocate it to either external or internal growth. Shipbuilding, leather goods and fur, clothing and footwear, timber and furniture, building construction and miscellaneous services are the orders not represented in either sample.

It should be noted that, because of differences in the column totals, some difference between the elements in each column must occur. The differences are however small, the maximum being three in Orders V, VI and XVI. The miscellaneous category, other manufacturing, clearly cannot have had any general forces making for or against mergers. In metal manufacture, the six trades of 1951 and the three products of 1958 all expanded externally; thus some under-representation of this industrial order in 1958 might explain a very minor portion of the discrepancy between findings. Finally, in engineering and electrical goods, the 1958 sample has more products than the 1951 sample. Curiously, all three of the 1951 trades are in the external-expansion group, and all but one of the six 1958 products are internally expanding. One might reasonably have expected that the larger representation of 1958 would pick up any general influences promoting mergers in the industry, but it has not.

The importance of vertical and horizontal mergers

A second possible source of discrepancy is the wider scope of a 1951 'trade' than of a 1958 'product'. For example, a starch firm producing modified starches could acquire a firm producing raw starch from maize, and this acquisition could be considered vertical under the 1958 definitions and horizontal in 1951. Thus, some of the leading firms in the highly concentrated trades in 1951 might have achieved their dominant positions by mergers which would be regarded as horizontal by Evely and Little, but which must be regarded as vertical in terms of the narrower 1958 definition of products. To produce high concentration within 1958 products mergers have to be horizontal; vertical mergers do not affect 1958 product concentration ratios, but they may well have increased the 1951 trade concentration ratios. Thus we need to know how important vertical mergers were in the group of 1951 trades classified as growing externally.

Starch is one of the obvious candidates; although some of Brown and Polson's acquisitions could certainly be described as vertical, the most important mergers were horizontal. The same is true of seven other 1951 trades (spirit distilling, sugar and glucose, motorcycles, zinc, lead, tin, iron and steel tubes) where, although there were vertical mergers, the most important mergers were horizontal. In spirit distilling, the Distillers Company diversified into industrial spirits in the 1900s, while the British Sugar Corporation was a government sponsored amalgamation of beet sugar producers without refining interests. In motorcycles, the two major firms acquired some capacity in engines. In the non-ferrous metal trades and in iron and steel tubes, firms sometimes integrated forward into fabrication. However, in sugar and motorcycles the great preponderance of mergers were horizontal, while in spirit distilling, Distillers' many horizontal mergers in whisky have been amply documented.[1] Also, the 1963 Census of Production included fabricating within the product-mix of the non-ferrous metal trades.

These eight are the only trades discovered where vertical mergers assumed any importance at all, and in each case they were of minor importance in overall terms. In the remaining twenty-seven trades of the 1951 sample, vertical mergers were not important.

The role of the State

Another possible explanation is that the State's role in industry has changed over time. The State took an interest in combinations in the explosives trade during 1914–18 and after, and also encouraged the erection of new tinplate works just before and after the 1939–45 war. Beet sugar mergers were part of a 'statutory reorganisation of the sugar industry'[2] in the mid-1930s. The 1958 sample also picked up three cases of state intervention promoting mergers: tinplate again, steel sheet for the same reasons as tinplate, and dyestuffs, which is rather similar to the case of explosives. Thus the two samples did not differ on this point. It may be noted that, in the later sample, there are three cases of state intervention tending to limit new entry and thus promote high concentration. The three cases are the two telecommunications products, where non-competitive tendering was maintained into the 1960s, and data processing equipment, where the government agreements with IBM and Remington Rand tended to preserve the leadership of the two major British firms. After 1963, steel nationalisation and the activities of the IRC contributed some minor increases in concentration to already highly concentrated trades.

The conclusion for this part must be that state intervention to promote mergers occurred in both samples and does not explain the different findings.

The age of the technology

Evely and Little note that in six of their internal-growth trades (man-made fibres, razors, rubber tyres, mineral oil refining, photographic plates and films, and cinematograph film printing), or three quarters of those trades where internal expansion was the norm, patents or access to technical know-how had conferred leadership on the major firms.[3] Firms in these trades did not need to merge in order to achieve leadership. On the other hand, there were also nine trades where patents and know-

---

[1] See pp. 28–9 above, and the references cited there.
[2] Evely and Little, *Concentration in British Industry*, p. 119.
[3] Ibid. pp. 135–7. There is of course an element of judgement in isolating those cases where technical know-how has given leadership to a firm or a few firms. Every firm can claim that its

how gave firms an initial foot-hold in the trade and where mergers occurred subsequently.

Could it be the case that in the 1958 sample we have a collection of products with a preponderance of new technologies exclusive to the major firms? It transpires that no less than thirteen of the internal-expansion products of the 1958 sample contained firms which were able to exploit an exclusive technology. The frozen foods patents acquired from General Foods and Chivers and Sons allowed Unilever quickly to establish a commanding lead in British production. The know-how of American firms in crawler tractors is a second example.[1] Conversely, in only six of the external-expansion products did firms have specially exclusive knowledge (in dyestuffs, steel sheet, tinplate, gramophone records, safety glass and plaster products), which, nevertheless, had to be supplemented by mergers for market dominance to be achieved.

In total, in fifteen of the thirty-five 1951 trades, and in nineteen of the thirty-two 1958 products, access to exclusive knowledge promoted high concentration. Thus this privileged access was relatively more important in promoting high concentration without mergers in the later than in the earlier sample. That may mean simply that in the later sample a larger number of new products occur – products which, in terms of industrial history, have just been born – where the exclusive leadership of the few has yet to be eroded by imitators and where, therefore, the need for the leading firms to maintain their leadership by mergers has not yet become apparent.

The ages of the trades and products

There are other reasons why the age of a product is likely to be associated with a tendency for leading firms to experience mergers. For example, the older a product is, the more recessions the firms producing it have had to endure and the more imitations or near substitutes have been produced. Most important, the older a product is, the more likely is it to have been affected by the fashion for combinations around 1900 and the reconstructions during the recession of the early 1920s.[2]

Table 5.2 allocates each of the 1951 trades and the 1958 products to an age group – pre-1900, 1900–25, or post-1925 – depending upon when the

own home-bred gadgets are an exclusive technology. Thus the reader has to trust both the judgements made by Evely and Little and the judgements made here. Should he be sceptical he can refer to the sources noted in the case studies of chapters 3 and 4 above.

[1] The other products are coffee, synthetic rubber, detergents, ball and roller bearings, the two telecommunications trades, data processing equipment, flat glass, manufactured fuels and precious metals refining. See also the previous footnote.

[2] On these see Utton, 'Some features of the early merger movements'; Fitzgerald, *Industrial Combination in England*; D. H. MacGregor, *Industrial Combination*, London, Bell, 1906; A. F. Lucas, *Industrial Reconstruction and the Control of Competition: the British experiments*, London, Longmans Green, 1937.

Table 5.2.   *The samples of high-concentration trades and products classified into age groups[a]*

	Trades (1951)[b]		Products (1958)[c]	
	Externally expanding	Internally expanding	Externally expanding	Internally expanding
Pre-1900	Bicycles	Photographic plates and	Blended whisky	Ball and roller bearings
	Cast iron pipes	films	Dyestuffs[h]	Cigars
	Cement	Rubber tyres and tubes[g]	Gin	Condensed and
	Cotton thread		Steel sheet	evaporated milk
	Explosives		Tin	Flat glass
	Fertilisers		Tinplate	Precious metals refining
	Floorcoverings		Wallpaper	Rubber tyres and tubes[g]
	Incandescent mantles			Soups[i]
	Iron and steel tubes			
	Lead			
	Margarine[d]			
	Matches			
	Salt mines			
	Soap and glycerine			
	Spirit distilling			
	Spirit rectifying			
	Starch			
	Sugar and glucose[e]			
	Tin			
	Tinplate			
	Tobacco			
	Transmission chains[f]			
	Wallpaper			
	Weighing machinery			
	Zinc			
41	25	2	7	7
1900–25	Asbestos cement goods	Cinematograph film	Asbestos cement goods	Cars
	Motorcycles	printing	Gramophone records	Data processing
	Valves and cathode ray tubes[j]	Ice cream[k]	Plaster products	equipment[m]
		Man-made fibres	Safety glass	Fish and marine
		Mineral oil refining		animal oils
		Razors[l]		Ice cream[k]

				Total	Example products (with count)
20	5	4	—		Line apparatus; Manufactured fuels; Telegraph and telephone installations; Wheeled tractors[n] — 8
Post-1925 3	—	—	—		
6	0	0	0		Coffee extracts and essences[p]; Crawler tractors; Detergents; Frozen fish; Frozen vegetables; Synthetic rubber — 6
Total 28	7	11	21	67	

a By the date of first factory production in the United Kingdom, but see notes to individual products for doubtful cases.

b Evely and Little's sample of high-concentration trades (see p. 7 above).

c The products listed in tables 3.8 and 4.10.

d A few factories were established (in Cheshire, Southall and Scotland) during the 1890s.

e Beet sugar production in the United Kingdom dates from after 1914–18, but refining began before 1900.

f Bicycle chains were produced well before 1900 – motor chains after 1900.

g Bicycle tyre production was well established by 1900.

h Production in the United Kingdom was not on a large scale before 1914–18, but there were many mergers in the trade before 1900.

i 'Workshop' production dates well back into the 1810s, but large-scale canning started only in the 1920s and 1930s.

j Of these, cathode ray tubes are post-1925.

k The 'American' ice, which could be factory produced and stored for long periods, came to Britain in the early 1920s.

l King Camp Gillette built his first British factory at Leicester in 1909.

m The British Tabulating Machine Company started to assemble machines in the late 1900s.

n Ford started production at Dagenham in 1933, but earlier there were other much smaller producers.

p Liquid essences were produced in a factory-type operation in the second half of the nineteenth century, but powdered instant coffee, which accounts for an overwhelming proportion of sales, dates from just before 1939. Other coffee products are excluded from the census concentration ratio.

factory manufacture of the product concerned was first established in the United Kingdom. It is possible to question some of the placings but the broad picture is quite clear.

The various trades and products are also classified as externally or internally expanding. The totals suggest that the older the product or trade in terms of its factory manufacture in the United Kingdom, the more likely is it to be an external-expansion trade or product. Some seven of the twenty-eight external-expansion trades in the 1951 sample were affected by the early 'combination movement', while another eight were affected by the smaller scale combination movement of the 1920s and 1930s.[1]

Our reconciliation of the two sets of findings is thus fairly clear. The earlier sample contained a large number of trades where high concentration was a legacy of a particular period in British industrial history. High concentration in these trades was sought largely for the monopoly or oligopoly power that could be achieved if all, or the largest, manufacturers combined. In contrast, the 1958 sample, containing a higher proportion of relatively young products, with an as yet largely unshared reservoir of new technology, did not reflect so profoundly the earlier combination movements.

A POOLING OF RESULTS

A total pooling of the Evely and Little results with the present findings would be improper for two reasons. First, the samples overlap at certain points and double counting should be avoided. Secondly, the samples differ in some respects: the 1958 sample excluded products with sales of under £10 million in 1963, while certain trades of the 1951 sample had five-firm sales concentration ratios of below 90 per cent in 1958. Cinematograph film printing must also be excluded because the coverage had changed in the 1963 Census from that in 1951. Other trades have to be excluded from the pool because they are more broadly defined than the products of the 1963 Census.[2]

After this pruning, there remain some ten external-expansion trades and two internal-expansion trades from the 1951 sample which can be pooled with the 1958 sample to give an impression of the importance of external and internal growth in a fairly uniform larger sample. They are razors and man-made fibres (internal-expansion trades), and valves and cathode ray tubes, bicycles, salt, cotton thread, cast iron pipes, sugar and glucose, matches, motorcycles, floorcoverings (external-expansion trades),

---

[1] See Utton, 'Some features of the early merger movements', tables I and II.

[2] They are photographic plates and films, starch, explosives, soap and glycerine, iron and steel tubes, and mineral oil refining. The 1963 Census did in fact publish concentration ratios for subcomponents of the last three trades.

plus 'cigarettes', which were added because it seemed pointless to exclude the tobacco trade as a whole from the 1951 list simply because cigars appeared in 1958. The result is that just over half (55 per cent) of the pooled list expanded internally and just under half (45 per cent) expanded externally. That is, internal and external expansion were roughly equal partners in the process whereby high concentration evolved.

SUMMARY OF FINDINGS

This chapter has sought to reconcile two sets of findings, so that a balanced view of the contribution of internal and external growth to oligopolisation and monopolisation may emerge. It appears that the 1951 sample included a disproportionate number of trades affected by the early combination movements and, conversely, the 1958 sample included a disproportionate number of young, new-technology products. When the results of the two samples were pooled it was found that internal expansion promoted high concentration in just over half of the product markets. In effect, however, we may conclude that internal and external expansion have been about equally responsible for the promotion of monopoly, near-monopoly and tight oligopoly.

CHAPTER 6

THE IMPORTANCE OF MONOPOLY

This chapter places the earlier findings in perspective by estimating the proportion of manufacturing industry which is oligopolised or monopolised. The concentration ratio aids this assessment, but other factors enter into consideration, namely competition from imports, countervailing power, potential competition from new entrants, and competition from all other products. It will also be useful to record how many of these products have been, or are being, investigated by the Monopolies Commission, and what the conclusions of that body were for the products concerned.

THE EXTENT OF MONOPOLY AND OLIGOPOLY

A total of thirty-two products were surveyed in the 1958 sample, and it was decided in the last chapter that twelve trades from the 1951 sample could be regarded as products. These additional twelve are thus added to the thirty-two products because they had 1963 sales of over £10 million and because, from all available evidence, the leading five firms controlled over 90 per cent of sales. The sales of all forty-four products in 1963 came to roughly £3605 million,[1] which represented some 14 per cent of the total sales of principal products of all manufacturing industries reported in the 1963 Census.[2] If the six trades excluded at the end of chapter 5 because of their heterogeneity are in fact included, the proportion of sales oligopolised or monopolised increases slightly to 17 per cent.

These percentages do not, however, accurately measure the extent of monopolisation in British industry. On the one hand there is some double counting, which may produce an upward bias in the proportions; certain monopolised products are used as inputs to other monopolised sectors and will form part of the sales value reported by these latter sectors.[3] To

---

[1] The one product for which a sales figure was not given by the 1963 Census was cast iron pipes, but an estimate of sales is possible from the information on 'sales of characteristic products' for 'pressure pipes and fittings' and 'other pipes and fittings' – both subdivisions of iron castings (Census of Production 1963, part 39, table 2).

[2] For this purpose, the total sales of principal products by industry are used (Census of Production 1963, part 131, table 6) minus coalmining, construction, water, gas, electricity, and merchanted goods and canteen takings.

[3] There is also double counting in the denominator, so to some (unknown) extent the upward bias is offset.

overcome this problem, figures measuring the value added by each sector are required, and these are not available. On the other hand, the importance of monopolisation is understated to the extent that monopolised products are inputs to other production processes. Where the process results in a consumer product the welfare losses associated with the reduction of output and increase in price may, in principle, be estimated for that product alone. Where the product is a producer's good any allocative distortions which arise in its production may be carried over into the next stage of the production process, input prices will be higher than under competitive market structures, and this may ultimately be reflected in the quantities and prices of goods offered to consumers.

Whether the proportion of value added in British industry affected by monopoly or oligopoly in its product markets is above or below 14 per cent, it is clearly not insignificant. Moreover, large numbers of products with sales of under £10 million have been excluded from the measurement, and other products have been excluded which, although oligopolised, did not meet the criterion of a 90 per cent five-firm concentration ratio.[1]

In other contexts, it has been thought instructive to estimate what would be the welfare gain involved were oligopoly and monopoly conditions in industry to be eradicated.[2] These gains are expressed as proportions of gross national product and appear to be trivially small (rarely more than 2 per cent), not least because the measurements are concerned only with a portion of the welfare losses.[3] Such computations do not make the facts disappear entirely; a significant proportion of British manufacturing industry is oligopolised or monopolised. In the following sections we shall attempt to portray the environment in which these oligopolies and monopolies operate.

[1] On both points it is worth noting a Parliamentary Question and Answer of 6 April 1970: 'Mr Barnett asked the Secretary of State for Employment and Productivity if he will list the industries in which over half the market is controlled by one company or group . . .' Mr Dell replied: 'No comprehensive list is available and in any case the length of the list would depend on the definition of an industry adopted. But on the most recent information available to the Department, it is believed that at least half the market is in the hands of one company or group for the 156 commodities in the appended list.' This list is reproduced in appendix A.

[2] See A. C. Harberger, 'Monopoly and resource allocation', *American Economic Review*, vol. 44, May 1954, pp. 77–87; and, for a survey of the American studies in the field, F. M. Scherer, *Industrial Market Structure and Economic Performance*, Chicago, Rand McNally, 1971, chap. 17.

[3] Measurement of the increase in producers' surpluses obtainable because markets are monopolised is considered irrelevant. If producers' surpluses arising from monopolised selling activities were estimated, this would enable us to make a point about the *distribution* of income. Economics does not tell us to prefer one income distribution to another, whereas welfare losses from a reduction of output at the margin are sustained by society at large. When other losses attributable to monopolisation are added (for example, losses in efficiency due to insulation from competition) the total can amount to over 6 per cent of gross national product, as in Scherer's estimate for the United States (ibid. p. 408).

THE STATE OF TRADE, IMPORTS AND COUNTERVAILING POWER

All products compete for the disposable income of consumers and, even in a growing economy, this can mean that some products face a declining market. As demand decreases it may be supposed that the power of the producer to exploit his market position for private gain is lessened, though not removed entirely. Secondly, information on the concentration ratios used here to typify oligopoly and monopoly situations is restricted to sales of goods manufactured in the United Kingdom. If concentration ratios included imports it might be found that the market dominance of the leading concerns is illusory. Thirdly, buyers downstream from the producers of the goods in question, or government departments exercising surveillance over the industry, may represent sources of countervailing power which limit the dominance of oligopolists and monopolists, and may pass on concessions to final consumers.

The occurrence of these three restraining influences upon the leading firms is suggested in table 6.1. Certain qualifications concerning the import shares must be made immediately. The imports of fish oils are largely unrefined and do not compete with the major product of the British trade, refined fish oils. The same is true for sugar, where the share shown takes into account raw sugar imports. Imports of data processing equipment certainly include electronic equipment, whereas the British sales figures do not. Again, the real import share here is probably less than 10 per cent and, anyway, is controlled mainly by IBM, an American firm which produces machines in the United Kingdom. The latter point can also be made with regard to other products – frozen vegetables and fish, where the vast majority of imports are purchased by the leading frozen food manufacturers for sale as their own brands; matches, where the bulk of imports from Sweden are controlled by the British Match Corporation subsidiary, J. John Masters; valves and cathode ray tubes, where most imports are made by domestic manufacturers or sold to them;[1] cigars, where all the leading tobacco firms have links with importers. A similar point, though with rather less force, can be made about imports of ball and roller bearings.[2] The upper and lower estimates for man-made fibres depend upon one's view as to which imports are competitive with

[1] See Monopolies and Restrictive Practices Commission, *Report on the Supply of Electronic Valves and Cathode Ray Tubes*, pp. 80–6.

[2] Imports of ball bearings were increasing rapidly in 1971 and early 1972. Although the Japanese share of the British market reached a mere 5·7 per cent in 1971, British manufacturers then came to a mutually satisfactory arrangement with Japanese exporters, who agreed to reduce their exports to the United Kingdom in 1972 by 15 per cent on the 1971 quantity (see *Sunday Times*, 18 June 1972, p. 64; *Financial Times*, 21 June 1972, p. 4 and 15 September 1972, p. 4).

Table 6.1. *Some restraining influences on monopolies and oligopolies*

	State of the market 1960–70	Percentage of market for imports, 1963	Countervailing power[a]
Products from 1951 sample			
Bicycles	Declining	3·1	—
Cast iron pipes	Declining	0·3	Government
Cigarettes	Stagnant	0·5	—
Cotton thread	Declining	0·7	—
Floorcoverings	Declining	0·4	—
Man-made fibres	Expanding	5·3–7·8[b]	—
Matches	Declining	12·8	—
Motorcycles	Declining	31·8	—
Razors	Expanding	—	—
Salt mines	Expanding	3·9	—
Sugar and glucose	Stagnant	42·7[c]	Government
Valves and cathode ray tubes	Expanding	12·7	Makers of radio and TV sets
High-concentration products, 1958			
Asbestos cement goods	Expanding	3·0	—
Ball and roller bearings	Expanding	8·9	—
Blended whisky	Expanding	—	Brewers
Cars	Expanding	3·0	—
Coffee extracts and essences	Expanding	6·6	Retailing chains
Condensed and evaporated milk	Expanding	3·9	Retailing chains
Crawler tractors	Expanding	8·3	—
Detergents	Expanding	4·3	—
Dyestuffs	Expanding	15·3	—
Fish and marine animal oils	Expanding[d]	38·6	—
Frozen fish	Expanding	28·2	Retailing chains
Frozen vegetables	Expanding	17·4	Retailing chains
Gramophone records	Expanding	2·3	—
Ice cream	Expanding	—	Retailing chains
Line apparatus	Expanding	2·3	Post Office
Rubber tyres and tubes	Expanding	2·2	Car makers, etc.
Safety glass	Expanding	0·5	Car makers
Soups	Expanding	1·8	Retailing chains
Steel sheet	Expanding	10·0	Government
Synthetic rubber	Expanding	31·4	Tyremakers
Telegraph and telephone installations	Expanding	1·3	Post Office
Tin and tin alloys	Declining	18·4	British Steel Corporation
Wallpaper	Stagnant	4·5	—
Wheeled tractors	Expanding	0·5	—

[a] Monopsony, oligopsony or state agencies.
[b] Depending on which imports regarded as competitive.
[c] 3·1 per cent only if raw sugar imports are excluded.
[d] Output of whale oil has declined, but the other sub-components have expanded.

Table 6.1. (*cont.*)

	State of the market 1960–70	Percentage of market for imports, 1963	Countervailing power[a]
Non-disclosure products, 1958			
Cigars	Expanding	10·5	—
Data processing equipment	Declining	30·2	—
Flat glass	Expanding	8·9	—
Gin	Expanding	—	Brewers
Manufactured fuels	Expanding	0·2	—
Plaster products	Expanding	2·6	—
Precious metals refining	Expanding	3·6	Large overseas agencies
Tinplate	Expanding	0·2	Government; tin can makers

SOURCES: Census of Production 1963; Customs and Excise, *Annual Statement of Trade of the United Kingdom 1963*, vol. 1, London, HMSO, 1966.

products of the extrusion processes, but the difference involved is not crucial. Two of the import shares now seem significantly dated – synthetic rubber, where the share has decreased to below 30 per cent since 1963, and cars, where it has increased to above 10 per cent during the years 1970–2. The import share for precious metals refining is fairly meaningless. Any refined metals which enter the United Kingdom may be further refined and it is mainly a processing service trade, where it is difficult to decide whether overseas refiners effectively compete for business in a truly international market. Finally, if the latest import figures were analysed to take account of the enlargement of the European Economic Community, no doubt one or two changes would be made. But in many cases comparable market supply information does not exist and official post-1968 concentration ratios certainly do not.

As a suitable guideline, we may adopt 10 per cent or more of the market as significant import penetration. With the above qualifications about the individual products in mind, it would appear that only five products (dyestuffs, steel sheet, tin, cars and motorcycles) face significant import competition which is not controlled to a large extent by indigenous firms. For three of these products import penetration is in fact over 15 per cent.[1] It is naturally difficult to know in each case whether import competition acts as an effective check on the abuse of monopoly power. If import

[1] A recent (July 1972) ruling by the European Court suggests that imports of dyestuffs are not competitive (*Financial Times*, 15 July 1972, p. 11). The Court found evidence of price collusion by ten concerns supplying 80 per cent of the EEC dyestuffs market. Different price levels in five national markets could not be explained '. . . by differences in costs and charges bearing on the manufacturers in these countries.' Thus we are left with four products under the import constraint.

penetration is achieved, it is usually assumed that the foreign country is producing a cheaper product. It is beyond the scope of this paper to offer any evidence to the contrary, but even assuming that it is broadly correct, domestic producers are still protected by transport costs and, in most cases, by tariff or non-tariff barriers of many kinds. This means that competition from the foreign producer is watered down. Consequently import competition does not always ensure that there is no abuse of monopoly power, even though it is likely to prevent its full exploitation.

The entries in the last column of table 6.1 are a starting point for discussion and not a judgement of the significance of countervailing power. Scherer has discussed countervailing power in the American economy and comes to a decidedly agnostic conclusion: 'Buyers *may* be able to exploit their power to secure lower intermediate product prices, and they *may* pass the resultant savings on to consumers.'[1] In the present context, where we are attempting judgements about forty-four specific products, there are twenty cases where some countervailing power might exist. The problem is to decide how significant countervailing power is – whether, for example, buying power is as concentrated as selling power – and, should it be significant, whether it may reasonably be supposed that the concessions won by buyers are passed on to consumers.

The food products may be eliminated at once. It might be thought that the buying power of supermarket chains which sell own-label products could extract concessions from the large food suppliers, but Jameson gives figures which suggest that such claims should be treated with some scepticism.[2] Buyer concentration in the retail grocery trade is quite low, as the figures in table 6.2 suggest. Moreover, own-label products are invariably manufactured by the dominant firms in each product group.

The brewers have accumulated some capacity in whisky and gin. In both cases their share of the trade is large enough for them to be considered dominant firms, but only in gin is production concentrated in one operation with one major brand. The production and selling of beer is in a few hands, and it does not appear that the brewers have used their production capacity as a lever to win concessions from whisky and gin producers. Rather, by instituting a system of financial incentives to house managers, they have concentrated on expanding the share of the market in their tied outlets.[3] Even if concessions are in fact won from producers, the selling of alcoholic drink as a whole is tightly oligopolised with, in addition,

---

[1] *Industrial Market Structure*, p. 252, Scherer's italics.

[2] E. Jameson, *Retailing in the Seventies*, London, J. Walter Thompson, 1970, pp. 1–3; see also Department of Trade and Industry, *Report of the Committee of Inquiry on Small Firms*, Cmnd 4811, London, HMSO, 1971, pp. 292–3. For a somewhat different view see W. S. Howe, 'Bilateral oligopoly and competition in the UK food trades', *Business Economist*, vol. 5, Summer 1973, pp. 77–87; Howe feels that food distributors have effective countervailing power, but doubts whether consumers benefit from it.   [3] On all these points see Monopolies Commission, *Beer*.

Table 6.2. *Retail grocery: shares of turnover by type of outlet,*
1969 and 1970

Percentages

	1969	1970
Multiples[a]	40·2	39·9
Co-operatives	15·4	15·3
Symbol independents	21·5	23·2
Other independents	22·9	21·6
Total	100·0	100·0

SOURCE: Jameson, *Retailing in the Seventies*, p. 3.
[a] In 1969 defined as having five branches or more; in 1970, ten or more.

each major brewer tending to concentrate regionally. It is doubtful whether, under these conditions, countervailing power benefits consumers.

Synthetic rubber production is dominated by a firm owned by the major tyremakers, the main users of synthetic rubber. Tyremaking appears in table 6.1 as a monopolised trade which, in turn, sells its product to car makers. This is also a monopolised product; and car makers purchase over 90 per cent of the safety glass produced.[1] Because the production of tyres, cars, bicycles, motorcycles and three-wheeled vehicles, tractors and aircraft are highly monopolised,[2] we cannot assume with certainty that concessions won from synthetic rubber, safety glass and tyre producers are likely to be passed on to consumers.[3]

A large proportion of smelted and refined tin is purchased by the British Steel Corporation, as a tinplate producer. But tinplate is a monopoly. Over half the tinplate sold in the home market is bought by one firm, Metal Box.[4] However, the top four firms in metal containers sold 85 per cent of marketed production in 1967 and 1968.[5] A few firms are able to extract concessions from the producers of metal containers, partly because they have installed their own capacity. These firms, notably Heinz, Nestlé and Carnation Foods, it will be remembered are among the

[1] Monopolies Commission, *Report on the Supply of Flat Glass*, para. 112.
[2] All but aircraft appear in table 6.1. The five-firm sales concentration ratio for aircraft increased from 86·6 to 98·0 per cent between 1958 and 1963.
[3] See *The Times*, 29 November 1971, p. 19, for an account of the exercise of countervailing power by car makers. The different profits earned in initial equipment and replacement markets by suppliers to the car industry are of interest here. In so far as it has been surmised that the countervailing power of car makers may be of little benefit to consumers, the fact that higher profits in replacement markets offset lower profits in initial equipment markets reinforces the point. For those who feel that the domestic car market is fiercely competitive, a study of D. G. Rhys, *The Motor Industry: an economic survey*, London, Butterworth, 1972, may give cause for a re-evaluation.
[4] Monopolies Commission, *Report on the Supply of Metal Containers*, HC 6, London, HMSO, 1970, para. 53.
[5] Ibid. para. 17.

dominant firms in soups, condensed and evaporated milk, and coffee,[1] products which appear in table 6.1. In any case, the Monopolies Commission failed to suggest that buyers of tin cans are as highly concentrated as the trade which sells them.[2]

Part of the refining of precious metals is performed for overseas firms and government agencies which place large individual orders. These firms and agencies may be able to extract concessions from British refiners to the extent that refining services are performed in an international market which is much less highly concentrated than the British market. However, British buyers of refining services are not very large, nor does any one of them buy a dominant share of refining services. The Bank of England has little call for refining services, as its requirements are for gold at standard purities and very little non-standard gold is imported. Demand for refined precious metals comes from many industries – dentistry, photography, and electronics being the chief purchasers. In so far as the concern here is to locate elements of countervailing power of benefit to British consumers, refining precious metals cannot be regarded as an example.

The dominant producers of valves and cathode ray tubes – Philips and Thorn – have vertically integrated into production of radio and television sets. Television sets are now a tight oligopoly, with Thorn and Philips having the two leading shares.[3] Radio sets are more competitive in terms of concentration of production, but the major valve suppliers are again vertically integrated – Thorn, Philips and GEC – so that the exercise of countervailing power is not called for.

Thus the discussion so far illustrates how few cases of effective countervailing power there are – effective in the sense of benefiting consumers. For countervailing power to be exercised, buyers must place individually large orders or have a large share in orders placed; if buyers place large orders it appears that they tend to have dominant selling positions in their own trades, thus reducing the incentive to pass on concessions won from their suppliers. Government agencies might wield a form of restraining power over some British monopolists, for example, in tinplate and steel sheet, while the dominant producer of cast iron pipes was also nationalised in 1967. The government has retained some overall powers of price restraint upon the British Steel Corporation,[4] but it is doubtful whether

[1] See chapter 3 above.

[2] See Monopolies Commission, *Report on the Supply of Metal Containers*, para. 133; the top four buyers who had come to 'agreements' with Metal Box accounted for 33 per cent of 'agreement' sales. 'Agreement' sales accounted for 88 per cent of total sales by Metal Box.

[3] See Hart, Utton and Walshe, *Mergers and Concentration in British Industry*, pp. 43–8.

[4] Ministry of Power, *Steel Nationalisation*, Cmnd 2651, London, HMSO, 1965, para. 36: 'Although the nationalisation measure will not give the Minister any specific powers on prices, he can be expected to be concerned with questions of price policy in the nationalised iron and

these powers extend to fixing price ceilings for individual products; rather they are probably used to indicate a general rate of price increase which may help to contain inflation.[1] Moreover, none of the legislation fixes standards of quality, so that control over real prices of specific products would appear to be negligible. The same general point can be made with respect to sugar refining (although variations in sugar quality are probably small), where government has retained the power to fix profit margins on refining activity. Nevertheless, these powers would appear to be sufficient to control the worst excesses of monopoly power,[2] notwithstanding the fact that the British Sugar Corporation has been criticised by the Public Accounts Committee of the House of Commons for its slowness in adopting cost-saving technology.[3]

The other area where a state agency exercises countervailing power is in telecommunications. The Post Office buys equipment from the trade and is a monopsonist in the public sector. It sets prices for contracts after cost investigations based on the lowest-cost supplier, and has in the past imported equipment when it has been dissatisfied with the performance of the home industry.[4] Perhaps few will disagree with the judgement that the monopolist seller of telephone services passes on some concessions won from suppliers of exchange equipment and line apparatus. The new Post Office Corporation has financial targets set for it by the government – 8·5 per cent return on mean assets, raised to 10 per cent in 1970 in the telecommunication sector – and this system of targets could be a sufficient constraint on monopoly.[5]

Overall, it would appear that the producers of three products (sugar, telegraph and telephone installations, and line apparatus) are significantly constrained by downstream buyers or state agencies, and that the benefits of constraint are passed on to consumers at least in some measure.[6]

Finally, eight products are declining, namely bicycles, cast iron pipes, cotton thread, floorcoverings, matches, motorcycles, tin and data processing equipment. The difficult problem here is to decide in which cases decline in the market could be an effective constraint on the exercise of monopoly power. The Monopolies Commission has found cases where

steel industry, in the same way that the responsible Ministers in successive Governments have been concerned with questions of price policy in the other nationalised industries.'

[1] See, for example, *Financial Times*, 10 October 1972, p. 42, where it is reported that the government is thinking in terms of a general '4 per cent price restraint policy.'

[2] See Hart, Utton and Walshe, *Mergers and Concentration in British Industry*, pp. 75–7.

[3] *Financial Times*, 27 May 1972; *Economist*, 3 June 1972, p. 78.

[4] See Hart, Utton and Walshe, *Mergers and Concentration in British Industry*, pp. 107–13 and the references cited therein; also *Guardian*, 3 July 1972, p. 16.

[5] Post Office, *Report and Accounts for the 6 months ended March 31 1970*, HC 155, London, HMSO, 1970, 'Introduction'.

[6] Admittedly the 'universal' price 'restraint', which was the aim of official policy in 1973, could have some relevance for the discussion, but this issue should be the subject of a separate study.

firms producing in static or declining markets have acted against the public interest, notably in calico printing, linoleum, matches, and cast iron rainwater goods. Even if the behaviour of a monopolist promises to hasten the demise of his product, in that his price and output policy encourages consumers to switch their expenditure even more rapidly to competing products, it could still be the case that this process is a drawn-out and lengthy one. The longer the process of exit, the greater are the welfare losses imposed on society. In this survey it is only possible to indicate in a general way those products where the decline in demand cannot be expected to have deprived monopolists and oligopolists of control over their output and price decisions.

In the bicycle trade demand has periodically expanded against a long-term downward trend, as new products, especially the Moulton bicycle, have been introduced. The decline in the tin trade is compounded of an expansion in fabricated tin products, especially solder, and a decline in tin smelting.[1] Data processing equipment and cotton thread are both trades where new products have been substituted for old, but where the major firms have dominant interests in the new products. Under such conditions producers are presumably less disposed to appease consumers of declining products. It may be unsafe to assume that the British Match Corporation is a significantly constrained monopolist in view of the findings of the Monopolies Commission, although, since the Commission reported, British Match has had to clear nominal price increases (including reductions in the number of matches in a box) with the Department of Trade and Industry.[2] However, this is not a constraint arising from the decline of the market, and the minor subtrade in firelighters is expanding.

For three products, namely cast iron pipes, motorcycles and floor-coverings, it seems reasonably plausible to suggest that declining demand could have significantly restrained the dominant firms, and, in one of these cases, motorcycles, the subtrade in three-wheeled vehicles is in fact expanding as new products have been introduced.[3]

In summary, the producers of some nine of the forty-four high-concentration products – cast iron pipes, floorcoverings, motorcycles, sugar, cars, line apparatus, steel sheet, telegraph and telephone installations, and tin – appear to encounter some measure of constraint upon their exercise of monopoly power. In addition, producers of cigarettes and

---

[1] Part of the decline in tin smelting may be explained by the switch of smelting to countries which mine the metal; Consolidated Tin Smelters, the largest British firm, has tin smelting interests in Nigeria and Australia.

[2] Monopolies and Restrictive Practices Commission, *Report on the Supply and Export of Matches*, paras. 193–227 and app. 5, p. 117. Production of matches stagnated after the war, while imports from Sweden (controlled by British Match) increased. On the other hand British Match does not control imports from Eastern Europe (less than 10 per cent of market supplies).

[3] This product group also faces significant import competition.

wallpaper could be said to operate in stagnant markets, but for a number of reasons we cannot regard stagnation in these markets as a serious restraining influence on oligopoly power. The Monopolies Commission has investigated the activities of the leading firms in both these trades and found them to be acting against the public interest.[1]

CONCENTRATION RATIOS AND COMPETITION

It has never been suggested that concentration ratios can describe all the elements which determine the degree of monopoly in a market for goods, and the previous section has considered the importance of some of the missing elements. Yet another objection to using concentration ratios as measurements of market power is that they may understate or overstate the dominance of leading firms. A five-firm ratio of 90 per cent, where the leading firm controls 80 per cent of sales and four others control 10 per cent between them, is an example of understatement; of more interest from our point of view is the case where the 90 per cent ratio is made up of five equal or roughly equal shares. In such cases, what are formally tight oligopolies could in fact be intensely competitive market structures. Less than a one fifth share of the market may not be a sufficient power base with which to exploit consumers of the product; on the other hand, it may be quite sufficient, given collusion, tacit or otherwise, on the part of the five major sellers.

It is not the purpose here to decide which of the forty-four products passes some arbitrary test of the intensity of competition. What can be done, however, is to look at the known facts about the distribution of firms' shares in each of the product markets to see whether the concentration ratio used to indicate monopolisation is seriously misleading. For this purpose some set of numbers must be used and the following are proposed: 50 per cent of sales for the leading firm, or 70 per cent for the two leading firms, or 80 per cent for the three leading firms. On this basis only five products have a distribution of market shares which is less skew than that proposed – crawler tractors, dyestuffs, fish oils, gramophone records and rubber tyres.

In view of the prevalence of highly skew distributions, it does not seem worthwhile following this line of objection to the use of concentration ratios. The use of a five-firm concentration ratio of 90 per cent to describe market monopolies or near-monopolies seems justified. It would be difficult to argue persuasively that the sample includes a large number of products where the concentration ratio understates the intensity of competition. There are, on the contrary, reasons why the concentration ratios published in the Census of Production tend to overstate competition

---

[1] See Hart, Utton and Walshe, *Mergers and Concentration in British Industry*, pp. 77–80 and 130–4.

in actual product markets. First, there is some degree of heterogeneity in the product groups listed in table 6.1; fish and marine animal oils are an obvious case, whilst in dyestuffs there is aggregation of different groups of colourants and bleaching agents. In both these examples, concentration is higher in the sub-markets making up the group in the Census of Production. Secondly, it is more apposite to think in terms of regional concentration ratios for some of the listed products which have a low value in relation to their weight or are perishable in transit; ice cream, manufactured fuels and sugar are three examples of this.

In summary, the concentration ratio used in this study does not appear to overstate the degree of concentration in actual product markets, rather the reverse. It is thus a useful indicator of monopoly or near-monopoly.

POTENTIAL COMPETITION

Bain has pointed out the limitation of looking merely to existing firms as sources of competitive pressure in a product market.[1] Potential new entry by as yet uncreated corporate entities, or others willing to diversify their activities, may also be a source of competitive pressure – so much so that these potential new entrants act as a constraint upon the oligopolistic or monopolistic power of existing firms. The problem has usually been to specify which of certain product markets have high entry barriers and for what reason. We cannot hope to go into such detail as Bain did for his selection of twenty products,[2] but there is much evidence on certain absolute entry barriers (patents and resource ownership) and other information which, taken with the work of Evely and Little on the fifty highly concentrated trades,[3] provides a picture of entry barriers for the forty-four products.

The overall position is shown in table 6.3. Trades to which footnote *a* refers were singled out by Evely and Little as having significantly high entry barriers. A few of the barriers described there have now been severely breached (for example, the 'ties with distributors' enjoyed by motorcycle manufacturers) and others in the table will probably go the same way; some of the barriers are not insurmountable and we do not have perfect foresight. Neither do we have perfect hindsight, but the past can teach us something about the height of entry barriers. There is no test like that of experience, so that we may take a suitable year, in this case 1958, and look for products where significant new entry has occurred over the period 1958–71. The meaning of 'significance' in this context needs to be defined. It cannot mean a *number* of firms, because they may

---

[1] Bain, *Barriers to New Competition.*
[2] Bain was, in most cases, able to get engineering estimates of scale–unit cost relationships (ibid. chap. 3).   [3] *Concentration in British Industry*, chap. IX.

Table 6.3.   *Entry barriers for the pooled samples of products*

Products from 1951 sample	
Bicycles[a]	Advertising; service and repair facilities; restrictive trading arrangements.
Cast iron pipes[ab]	Scale-economies; quotas fixed by rainwater goods trade association.
Cigarettes[abc]	Advertising; state import quotas; restrictive distribution arrangements; financing duty.
Cotton thread[a]	Capital costs.
Floorcoverings[ab]	Capital costs; distributive ties; other restrictive distribution arrangements.
Man-made fibres[abd]	Scale-economies; capital costs; patents; market-sharing agreement for rayon, 1937.
Matches[ab]	Capital costs; essential machinery; access to raw materials.
Motorcycles[ad]	Ties with distributors; other restrictive trading arrangements.
Razors[a]	Patents and technical know-how; advertising.
Salt mines[a]	Ties with distributors.
Sugar and glucose[a]	Scale-economies; capital costs; technical know-how; state production quotas.
Valves and cathode ray tubes[ab]	Scale-economies; patents and technical know-how; restrictive distribution arrangements.
High-concentration products, 1958	
Asbestos cement goods[a]	Scale-economies; access to raw materials; distributive linkages and other restrictive arrangements.
Ball and roller bearings[a]	Scale-economies; patents.
Blended whisky[a]	State licensing regulations; advertising.
Cars[cd]	Scale-economies; advertising; capital costs; technical and design know-how.
Coffee extracts and essences	Technical know-how; advertising.
Condensed and evaporated milk	Capital costs; advertising.
Crawler tractors	Technical know-how; patents.
Detergents[bd]	Patents and technical know-how; advertising.
Dyestuffs	Technical know-how; R and D expenditure.
Fish and marine animal oils	Capital costs; technical know-how; access to raw materials (vertical integration).
Frozen fish	Patents; advertising; distributive linkages.
Frozen vegetables	Patents; advertising; distributive linkages.
Gramophone records	Patents and technical know-how; scale-economies; vertical integration.
Ice cream[a]	Capital costs; hygiene regulations; service facilities; refrigeration supplies.
Line apparatus	State tendering arrangements; patents and technical know-how; capital costs; R and D expenditure.

Table 6.3. (cont.)

Rubber tyres and tubes[a b c]	Patents; access to raw materials; vertical integration downstream; advertising.
Safety glass[b]	Patents and technical know-how; capital costs; scale-economies; vertical integration.
Soups	Advertising.
Steel sheet	Scale-economies; technical know-how; vertical integration; state quotas.
Synthetic rubber	Capital costs; vertical ties with buyers; scale-economies; technical know-how.
Tin and tin alloys	Capital costs; technical know-how; vertical integration.
Telegraph and telephone installations	State tendering arrangements; patents and technical know-how; capital costs; installation economies; R and D expenditure.
Wallpaper[a b]	Capital costs; distributive linkages, and other restrictive practices.
Wheeled tractors[c]	Scale-economies; patents and technical know-how; capital costs; advertising.
Non-disclosure products, 1958	
Cigars[a]	Advertising; state import quotas; financing duty.
Data processing equipment	Patents and technical know-how; R and D expenditure.
Flat glass[b c]	Patents and technical know-how; capital costs; scale-economies; vertical integration.
Gin[a]	State licensing regulations; advertising; technical know-how.
Manufactured fuels	Patents and technical know-how; scale-economies; vertical integration.
Plaster products[c]	Patents and technical know-how; access to raw materials.
Precious metals refining[a]	Patents and technical know-how; links with mines and state trading bodies; scale-economies.
Tinplate[a]	Scale-economies; technical know-how; vertical integration; state quotas.

[a] Entry barriers to these trades discussed in Evely and Little, *Concentration in British Industry*, chap. IX. For bicycles, cigarettes, floorcoverings, matches, sugar, ice cream, rubber tyres, wallpaper, cigars and tinplate these barriers '... appear to be most marked and ... their cumulative effects may be considerable' (p. 143).

[b] These entry barriers may be better understood by reference to the relevant reports of the Monopolies Commission.

[c] These products considered in H. M. Mann, 'Seller concentration, barriers to entry and rates of return in thirty industries, 1950–60', *Review of Economics and Statistics*, vol. 48, 1966, pp. 296–307. Of the above products Mann classified barriers as 'very high' for cigarettes, cars and flat glass, 'substantial' for wheeled tractors and 'moderate to low' for rubber tyres (where the much larger American market probably explains the discrepancy with the position in this country).

[d] These products are considered in Pratten, *Economies of Scale in Manufacturing Industry*, where estimates of their minimum efficient plant size are expressed as percentages of the British market. The reciprocals of these shares, i.e. the number of producers of minimum efficient scale that the market will support, are man-made fibres (6), motorcycles (10), cars (1 or 2) and detergents (5).

have achieved only a tiny market share by taking up residence in a very
specialised segment of the market. Thus, if only one firm enters but takes
20 per cent of the market, this may be described as significant new entry.
To be consistent with the kind of benchmark used above, we shall take
10 per cent of market penetration by firms entering the market after 1958
as significant new entry.[1] This amounts to requiring an average increase
in the collective market share of new entrants of less than 1 percentage
point per annum over the period.

In only four of the forty-four products has new entry been able to
achieve that measure of success. The products, with the entrants in
question, are bicycles (Moulton), crawler tractors (Caterpillar and Case),
soups (Campbell's and others), synthetic rubber (Doverstrand and oil
companies). In addition, new entrants to the gramophone record industry
have achieved just under 10 per cent penetration, while, if CBS's expansion of the old Oriole Company's facilities is recognised as new entry and
not merely the growth of an existing company,[2] the list swells to five.
However, it seems quite inappropriate to have such a young product as
synthetic rubber in the list, because manufacture was hardly established
in the United Kingdom by 1958. Omitting this product gives us four cases
only of significant new entry since 1958.

Unfortunately such evidence only allows us to conclude that entry
barriers for these products were not such as to actually forbid entry. It does
not allow us to conclude that entry barriers were forbiddingly high in the
remaining trades. Entry barriers may have been moderately low in the
remaining trades, while the resident manufacturers could have staved
off potential new entry with a variety of strategies. Nevertheless, it would
seem specious to argue that a combination of low entry barriers *and* entry-
forestalling strategies did not have the same effect as high entry barriers.
Another point to be made here is that some of the remaining products
were declining and we do not expect new entry in declining markets.
An exception to that rule was bicycles, where new entry did occur as the
result of product innovation.[3]

---

[1] Even if the new firms were subsequently acquired by other firms in the industry, the contribution of new entrants can thus be gauged.

[2] This introduces an extra element of judgement into the discussion; the same judgement
has not been made regarding ICI's acquisitions in the wallpaper trade. Similarly, Fafnir Bearing
may have 10 per cent or more of the ball bearing trade, but much of the share derives from the
acquisition of Fischer Bearings. In valves and cathode ray tubes, RCA Colour Tubes, which is
now controlled by Thorn, entered after 1958 but only controlled 6 per cent at most of trade sales
when acquired by Thorn. In coffee, Sol Café expanded its share of trade sales to above 10 per
cent after its acquisition by Lyons in the mid-1960s; before this Sol Café had no manufacturing
plant in the United Kingdom.

[3] Cf. Pratten, *Economies of Scale in Manufacturing Industry*, pp. 157–61; this account of scale-
economies in bicycle manufacture notes that the trade has promoted the notion of following a
fashion – the type of competitive environment in which new entrants may flourish.

THE MONOPOLIES COMMISSION

One other obvious constraint upon the behaviour of monopolists is the existence of the Monopolies Commission. The Commission has investigated twelve of the forty-four products surveyed here. Cellulosic fibres was the subsector of man-made fibres investigated; flat glass and safety glass were investigated together; the others were wallpaper, tyres, valves and cathode ray tubes, linoleum, cast iron rainwater goods, matches, detergents, cigarettes, and asbestos cement. Only Pilkington, the maker of the two glass products, was not, in some form or other, found to be acting against the public interest. Thus, while Pilkington was found to be a benevolent monopolist, other firms were singled out for criticism – Courtaulds, Imperial Tobacco, WPM, the British Match Corporation, Unilever, Procter and Gamble, and Turner and Newall. In the remaining four cases (rubber tyres, valves and cathode ray tubes, linoleum, cast iron rainwater goods) the trade as a whole was criticised.

How much of a constraint the Commission has been upon oligopolists and monopolists is open to question. There is no formal follow-up procedure within the Commission itself to determine how far recommendations supported by the Minister are acted upon. There are scraps of evidence to go on – WPM has not acquired any more firms in the trade since the Commission found against its acquisition policy (it has itself been acquired by Reed International); Imperial Tobacco has divested itself of its holding in Gallaher and discontinued its retailer bonus system; in valves and cathode ray tubes the Commission would have found against the trade but for the fact that its anti-competitive practices had been discontinued before judgment was given. Furthermore, without a follow-up procedure it is not possible to know whether new devices have been substituted for old in order to circumvent the Commission's criticisms.

It may be supposed that, once a product is investigated, there exists some incentive within the management of the companies concerned to avoid being called upon again to explain and justify their behaviour. Also, the firms concerned may have given undertakings to the Department of Trade and Industry which amount to a constraint on their ability to exploit their market power.

SUMMARY OF FINDINGS

In this chapter the constraints upon monopolists and near-monopolists have been discussed. The sources of competition to existing manufacturers were all other goods (where the trade is declining in an expanding economy), imports and potential new entrants. Furthermore, we have

discussed whether other external constraints confronting manufacturers –
sources of countervailing power or the Monopolies Commission – tend to
dilute their market power. There was also a section on the nature of the
typical market-share distribution of firms under the product headings.
There, it was decided that the concentration ratio used was not seriously
misleading and indicated fairly the areas where monopoly or tight
oligopoly could be assumed to exist in some degree.[1]

The results of the survey may be summarised as follows.

(1) Manufacturers of four products faced substantial import competition.

(2) Manufacturers of three products were probably constrained by
declining demand.

(3) Manufacturers of three products faced effective countervailing
power which benefited consumers.

(4) Four products experienced significant new entry over the period
1958–72.

(5) Twelve products have been investigated by the Monopolies Commission.

If all these products were eliminated from the sample of forty-four,
twenty-two would remain – cotton thread, man-made fibres (non-
cellulosic), razors, salt mines, ball and roller bearings, blended whisky,
coffee, condensed and evaporated milk, dyestuffs, fish and marine animal
oils, frozen fish, frozen vegetables, ice cream, synthetic rubber, wheeled
tractors, cigars, data processing equipment, gin, manufactured fuels,
plaster products, precious metals refining and tinplate. None of these
has yet been investigated by the Monopolies Commission, although
plasterboard was referred in September 1972. While two are in declining
markets (data processing equipment and cotton thread), it was argued
above that falling demand could not necessarily be interpreted as a
significant constraint upon the dominant firms. The remaining twenty
products are in expanding markets; none of them faces significant import
competition and there have not been any important new entrants to
these trades over the period 1958–71 (with the exception of synthetic
rubber which, however, was only established as a trade in the United
Kingdom in the mid-1950s). While the producers of synthetic rubber and
tinplate may be constrained by large buyers of their output, it has been
argued that these constraints probably do little to benefit consumers
because the buying trades too are highly monopolised.

The discussion in appendix B below suggests that two other products –
primary batteries and accumulators – could be added to the above list.

---

[1] It remains to be argued whether an exercise to determine the 'real' intensity of competition
could be carried out except in the context of a full-scale Monopolies Commission inquiry.
Moreover, Monopolies Commission inquiries do not always produce a unanimous report.

These were two of the fourteen products excluded from Evely and Little's discussion on the emergence of high concentration. One of them, accumulators, has been investigated by the Monopolies Commission,[1] while the other is currently under investigation.

It is best to conclude this chapter with a reminder about certain products that have escaped our attention; in each case they may be included in the list of monopolised and oligopolised products in appendix A.

(1) The concentration levels of some products were still below 90 per cent in 1958 although they had reached that level by 1963.

(2) Some products are produced under tight oligopoly conditions but still do not qualify under the criterion of 90 per cent concentration.

(3) Some products do not qualify because their sales were below £10 million in 1963.

(4) The Census of Production gives incomplete information on some products; either they are given a concentration ratio for 1963 but not for 1958, or aggregation of products has concealed monopolisation.

Finally, very little is known about regional monopolies; concentration may be low on a national basis while being very high in separate regions. Evidently the above discussion must be regarded as a first step in a survey of monopolised products in British industry.

[1] *Report of the Supply of Electrical Equipment for Mechanically Propelled Land Vehicles*, HC 21 London, HMSO, 1963.

CHAPTER 7

CONCLUSIONS

SUMMARY OF FINDINGS

This book started out with three aims:

(i) to ascertain the relative importance of internal and external growth in promoting monopoly and near-monopoly;

(ii) to show whether monopoly or near-monopoly was durable;

(iii) to assess the constraints on the exercise of monopoly and oligopoly power.

The findings on (ii) are reported first.

A government policy on monopolies would be redundant if monopoly power were a temporary matter, always rapidly eroded by new competition. However, the findings of chapter 2 show that permanent monopoly surveillance is required. In that chapter, a survey of thirty-six trades, initially categorised by Evely and Little as high-concentration trades in 1951,[1] revealed that in thirty-two cases monopoly and oligopoly had proved durable. Twenty-five of the trades had experienced an increase in concentration after 1951 up to the late 1960s. In another seven cases no perceptible change had occurred. Thus, the instances where monopoly or tight oligopoly had shown a tendency to dissolve were very few.

A second and related finding in chapter 2 was that mergers were often used to buttress or further entrench the monopoly and oligopoly market power achieved by 1951. In only eight of the thirty-six trades could no evidence of merger activity since 1951 be discovered. Most of the firms which had grown internally up to 1951, that is to say without merger activity, used external growth as a means of increasing their market power after that date.

Unfortunately we cannot make a quantitative assessment of the importance of mergers in these trades after 1951. All that can be said is that certain mergers took place and that, at a date in the late 1960s or early 1970s, concentration stood at such and such a (usually higher) level. It is not possible to conclude that mergers caused the increases in concentration, because they may have played a subsidiary role compared with internal growth in maintaining high concentration in the trades surveyed.

Evely and Little's major finding on the roles played by internal and external growth in promoting high concentration was: 'There are few firms indeed among the leaders in the trades surveyed which were not

---

[1] *Concentration in British Industry*, chap. VIII.

created by an amalgamation or have not resorted to acquisition and merger at some stage during their development.'[1] In the light of their conclusion and of our findings on the durability of high concentration after 1951, the machinery of monopoly surveillance could very easily become entirely preoccupied with the scrutiny of monopoly positions achieved by mergers. This would be regrettable, because chapters 3 and 4 showed that most monopoly positions have in fact been obtained by internal growth.

A total of thirty-two products was surveyed in chapters 3 and 4. The twenty-four products surveyed in chapter 3 were all those for which the 1963 Census of Production published five-firm sales concentration ratios for 1958 of 90 per cent or more. The eight products discussed in chapter 4 are of special interest as examples of classic monopoly, duopoly and tri-opoly. They have not previously been analysed because concentration is so high in these product markets that the confidentiality rules of the Census have prevented the disclosure of the relevant information by official sources.

Eleven of the thirty-two products considered became monopolies or near-monopolies as a result of merger activity. In the majority of cases surveyed here, high concentration is explained by internal growth of a few firms which has eliminated the competition of many others, or by the fact that few firms have ever entered production of the commodity in question. Nevertheless, in ten of the thirty-two cases mergers were an important tool used to prevent the erosion of market shares once market power had been obtained by internal growth.

These findings are not inconsistent with one interpretation of Evely and Little's findings (see the quotation from page 129 above). That is, if Evely and Little merely wanted to suggest that in most high-concentration trades mergers were experienced either in the process of promoting high concentration or during some later phase in development, then our findings give a broad measure of support to that suggestion.

However, another interpretation is possible – that in most high-concentration trades mergers were responsible for promoting monopoly or tight oligopoly. Indeed, as chapter 2 seeks to show, the data used by Evely and Little strongly support this finding, because in twenty-eight of the thirty-six trades surveyed it was clear that mergers had played the major role in achieving high concentration. Thus, it became necessary to investigate why the two sets of data used – the thirty-six trades surveyed by Evely and Little, and the thirty-two products surveyed here – yielded different answers to the question of whether external growth is relatively more important than internal growth in promoting monopoly or tight oligopoly.

[1] Ibid. p. 129.

Chapter 5 reconciled the two answers. The reason for the difference in findings had very little to do with three of the possible sources of divergence that were examined. First, the two samples had broadly similar representation in the industrial orders, so that any particular influences operating within certain industries would have been reflected in both. Secondly, Evely and Little's survey was one of trades rather than products, and therefore might be thought to include an inordinate number of cases where vertical mergers took place, but that factor was of very little significance. Thirdly, changes in the role of the State only explained a very minor part of the difference in findings. The explanation of the difference was eventually attributed to technological bias – Evely and Little's sample included a large number of old-technology trades, whereas our sample contained a greater number of younger, new-technology products. Evely and Little's sample was derived from the 1951 Census of Production and their sample trades had all been established by 1935, a date which they used to measure changes in concentration up to 1951; our sample used an initial date of 1958. Perhaps it was thus inevitable that new-technology products would be found in the later sample and not in the earlier. The older trades were more likely to have been affected by the waves of combinations to suppress competition in times of excess capacity which prevailed shortly before and at the turn of the present century, and again during the 1920s. Firms exploiting the relatively newer technologies of the later sample had no need to resort to mergers. The market power which their access to new technology had conferred upon them precluded the development of effective competition, at least over the period studied here.

While the above certainly helps to establish the importance of mergers in producing monopoly power, it does not put monopoly power itself into its proper perspective. For some product markets there exist potential constraints upon the monopolist such that he may never be fully able to exploit his nominal market power. Chapter 6 makes an exploratory contribution to this area of discussion, using forty-four products as the test data.[1] The aim was to discover to what extent monopoly or tight oligopoly power may be regarded as serious and, also, where it may be fairly ignored in all the circumstances.

Five types of constraint were considered: monopolists and oligopolists may encounter significant import competition which is not controlled by themselves; or they may be operating in rapidly declining markets, and thus find themselves unable to extract monopoly rents from consumers who are deserting the product. These two factors were significant for

[1] The data were the thirty-two products of chapters 3 and 4, and twelve of Evely and Little's trades which could properly be regarded as products and in all other respects similar to the products surveyed in chapters 3 and 4.

four and three products respectively out of the total of forty-four. For three other products countervailing power could have been exercised for the benefit of consumers; for a further four products there were low or moderately low entry barriers, which provided scope for potential competition and so constituted a constraint on the unbridled exercise of market power; finally, the Monopolies Commission had investigated twelve of the products, and it may reasonably be assumed that their surveillance has provided some kind of check on the exercise of monopoly or near-monopoly power. Some twenty-two products, just half of the cases examined, remained.[1] In these cases monopoly power is apparently a serious matter. These products faced little import competition; market decline did not constitute a check on the leaders' activities; there were high entry barriers encircling the producers; and there were no important sources of countervailing power pitted against them. None of these products has so far been investigated by the Monopolies Commission.

CERTAIN QUALIFICATIONS

The above study has proceeded without discussion of a number of important points. In the survey of constraints on monopolists and oligopolists, the existence of substitutes (on the demand side) to the products discussed has not been fully considered. This was partly because data from the Census of Production had to be used, and these are arranged on a production rather than a market basis. The reader will thus have to exercise ordinary caution in interpreting the findings of chapter 6. To some extent the existence of substitutes was recognised, in that the state of the trade for each product, whether it was expanding or contracting, was treated as a possible constraint upon monopolistic power.

Secondly, it must be repeated that nothing has been surmised about collusion, either in the trades examined here, or between the manufacturers of less concentrated products. Adam Smith may have been quite correct in claiming that the legal existence of trade associations, even a mere register of names of manufacturers in a trade, is enough to guarantee that producers are conspiring against the public. Collusion, market-sharing, quota agreements and so on may have been important in establishing or maintaining high concentration in some of the product markets surveyed. Without detailed and certain knowledge, preferably published in some widely available source, it is proper to suppress such elements from this discussion. The possibility of collusion between producers of

---

[1] Certain product monopolists were counted as being constrained under more than one heading, while only part of one product group had been investigated by the Monopolies Commission. Consequently, the numbers of products in this paragraph do not sum to forty-four.

products which are not very highly concentrated is important, because the level of concentration used in this study may be too high. By extending the net further, some less concentrated product markets, which are in fact collusive oligopolies, might have been included in the sample.

Again, it is worth reminding the reader of the special nature of the data: products with sales of under £10 million in 1963 were excluded by the Census; monopolised products which had been aggregated with other (monopolised or non-monopolised) products in the Census could not be considered; it is possible that some 'non-disclosure' products with sales of over £10 million in 1963 were not discovered; certain products for which the concentration information in the Census was incomplete or of a non-standard nature,[1] but which were certainly highly monopolised (mineral oil refining and aero-engines are cases in point), could not be considered.

In this matter, as in the matters of collusion and substitute products, the policy of the study has been to say nothing at all where what could be said was very little. Finally, as always, it has been necessary to use judgement in addition to techniques and facts in drawing conclusions on monopoly. These judgements are unbiased, though in some cases they may be subject to dispute. This is unavoidable, but at least such differences of opinion should indicate where, and in what forms, the monopoly problem is most pressing, and where an official Monopolies Commission investigation is most urgently required.

---

[1] For example, in a few cases concentration information was given for more than five firms, so that it was not possible to derive a five-firm sales concentration ratio.

MONOPOLISED AND OLIGOPOLISED PRODUCTS

The following list, published in *Hansard* for 6 April 1970, is of 156 products where one producer controlled over 50 per cent of United Kingdom supplies.

Baker's yeast
Cotton linters
Cellulose acetate tow
Man-made fibres[1]
Phosphorus
Soda ash
Hydrogen peroxide
Boric acid
Oxygen
Urea
Lithopone
Phosphates
Nylon polymer
Polyethylene terepthalate
Polytetrofluoroethylene
Rubber contraceptive goods
Rayon yarn
Plate and sheet glass
Unwrought nickel[2]
Magnesium metal
Gas cylinders, welded, low-pressure
Heavy safes and strong-room doors[2]
Lawn mowers
Hosiery and knitting machinery
Motor scrapers
Non-electric carpet sweepers
Mustard
Rayon staple fibre
Salt, industrial and rock[1]
China clay
Phosphoric acid
Calcium carbide

Refined borax
Pyridine
Dissolved acetylene
Ammonium carbonate and bicarbonate
Nitrogenous fertilisers[2]
Sporting cartridges
Polymethyl methacrylate
Celluloid
Casein plastics
Wallpaper[1]
Metallic yarn
Iron pressure pipes and fittings
Unwrought zinc[2]
Gas cylinders, seamless, high-pressure
Wood screws
Precision chains
Tufted carpet machinery
Boot and shoe machinery
Weighing machinery
Diaphragm valves
Ignition coils, magnetos, distributors, ignition suppressors for motor vehicles
Windscreen wiper motors
Lamps, horns, trafficators, relay units for motor vehicles
Automatic transmissions for motor vehicles
Universal joints for transmission systems

[1] The 1963 Census of Production published concentration ratios for these twenty products.

[2] The 1963 Census of Production included these twenty products in larger groups of products for which concentration ratios were published.

Shock absorbers
Fuel injection equipment for diesel engined vehicles
Bicycles[2]
Speedometers
Heater devices for motor vehicles
Matches
Drop forged crankshafts
Tyre valves
Basic slag
Certain frozen foods[1]
Soups[1]
Cereal breakfast foods[1]
Canned peas[2]
Canned baked beans[2]
Sugar[1]
Margarine[1]
Vinegar
Whisky[1]
Gin
Cigarettes and tobacco[1]
Refined petroleum products[1]
Caustic soda
Chlorine
Glycerine
Dynamos, current-voltage control units, starter motors for motor vehicles
Door locks and fittings for motor vehicles
Methanol
Polypropylene
Soap[1]
Synthetic detergents[1]
Potash
Gelatine and glue[1]
Polyethylene
Cellulose film[1]
Asbestos goods[1]
Safety glass[1]
Brass 'semis' (extruded)[2]
Nickel alloy 'semis'[2]
Metal containers[1]

Wire rope
Diamond dies
Oil well drilling bits
Crown corks
Needles[2]
Pistons and piston rings
Brake linings and clutch facings
Plasterboard
Cylinder block castings
Stencil duplicators
Punched-card machinery
Cash registers
Steel works plant
Bearings and bushes for motor vehicles[2]
Sewing machines, domestic and industrial
Grain milling machinery
Excavators
Road rollers
Towed scrapers
Dish washers
Packaging machinery
Tonnage oxygen plants
Rubber-working machinery
Tobacco machinery
Brushmaking machinery
Vacuum cleaners[2]
Electricity house service meters
Gas welding equipment
Fire and burglar alarms
Dry (primary) batteries[2]
Electrical instruments for motor vehicles[2]
Sparking plugs, compression ignition heater plugs
Electronic valves[2]
Cathode ray tubes[2]
Semi-conductors[2]
Carburettors for cars
Tanning and leather working machinery
Drum and disc brakes

[1] The 1963 Census of Production published concentration ratios for these twenty products.
[2] The 1963 Census of Production included these twenty products in larger groups of products for which concentration ratios were published.

Overdrives, line drive shafts

Steering gears for vehicles

Steering wheels

Timing chains

Clutches

Petrol tanks and axle casings

Caravans[2]

Rubber footwear[1]

Cinematographic equipment

Parking meters

Photographic film

Electric clocks

Brass band instruments

Mechanical lighters

Fuel lift pumps for vehicles

Engine valves for vehicles

Bottled gas

Oil seals for vehicles

Razors (safety) and razor blades[2]

Nylon yarn

Linoleum[2]

Cement[1]

Among the products missing from this list we may note paper-making machinery, cod liver oil, incandescent mantles, steel sheet, tinplate, tin and three-wheeled vehicles.

[1] The 1963 Census of Production published concentration ratios for these twenty products.

[2] The 1963 Census of Production included these twenty products in larger groups of products for which concentration ratios were published

APPENDIX B

THE FOURTEEN TRADES OMITTED FROM
EVELY AND LITTLE'S SAMPLE

As mentioned in chapter 2, Evely and Little's survey of highly concentrated trades was illustrative rather than comprehensive. In fact, fourteen of the original fifty trades were not discussed. It is of interest to see whether any of these fourteen qualify for inclusion among the monopolised products considered in chapters 3 to 6 and, if so, whether their inclusion modifies the results in any way.

They were primary batteries; accumulators; vinegar and other condiments; wholesale bottling of wines and spirits; precious metals refining; small arms; prime movers (internal combustion); abrasive wheels; tramways, trolleybuses and omnibuses; ball and roller bearings; cast iron stoves and grates (other); boilers and boilerhouse plant; notepaper, pads and envelopes; asbestos manufactures.

Two of these trades (ball and roller bearings and precious metals refining) *were* considered in chapters 3 and 4. Two further trades (wholesale bottling and trams, etc.) may be excluded here because they were excluded from the 1958 Census as a result of changes in coverage. Another two trades (small arms and vinegar) had sales of less than £10 million in 1963, so that, as with other of the 1951 trades, we may properly exclude them from consideration. For four of the trades (prime movers, boilers, asbestos and abrasive wheels) the 1963 Census gave five-firm concentration ratios which were below 90 per cent in 1958.

Information outside the Census makes it possible to conclude that the concentration ratios for two other products (cast iron stoves and grates, and notepaper, etc.) did not reach 90 per cent in 1958. The latter barely passed Evely and Little's criterion of 67 per cent, with a three-firm concentration ratio by net output of 68 per cent in 1951. It appears from one source that this product group is dominated by five concerns (John Dickinson, Wiggins Teape, Spicers, Harold Wesley and Newton Mill),[1] who together account for about 70 per cent of sales, while the remainder is accounted for by 130 or so smaller concerns.

The case of cast iron stoves and grates (other than appliances using coal or other solid fuel), is rather similar. In 1951 the three-firm concentration ratio by net output was 69 per cent. The major firms in the trade in 1951 were Allied Ironfounders, R. and A. Main, and Radiation, all of whom had built up interests in the gas-fired iron castings appliance industry by means of acquisition.[2]

[1] *The UK as a Market for Printing and Writing Papers*, Business Intelligence Services, London, 1970, p. 98.
[2] The products were gas cookers, gas fires and gas water heaters. All three companies were eventually acquired by larger concerns in the 1960s: Allied by Glynwed, R. and A. Main (later Glover and Main) by Thorn, and Radiation by Tube Investments.

This subsector of the trade was responsible for 70–5 per cent of sales in 1951. Electrically powered appliances, which made up a mere 12·6 per cent of sales in 1951, took a much larger share of output by 1958,[1] and the trade in electric cookers dominated the subsector. According to one source the top five firms in electric cookers controlled only 74 per cent of sales in 1962 and the firms involved (Belling, Tube Investments, Radiation, English Electric, Tricity Cookers) were, with one exception, not of any importance in the gas appliance sector.[2] Over the period 1951–8, cast iron gas and electric cookers ceded their market position to models constructed from sheet steel, and foundries were, by 1958, mainly supplying cast iron parts (burners, plates and frames) to both the gas and electric subsectors. The only sector to lag behind these developments was the catering equipment trade, where five foundries dominated – Allied Ironfounders, Carron and Company, Benham and Sons (a subsidiary of Glover and Main), Marwood (Blackburn), and Smith and Wellstood. Others of some importance in the trade were Cannon Industries, Sidney Flavel, Stoves of Liverpool, Valentines and Valor in gas cookers, and Federated Foundries, GEC and Cannon in electric cookers. Altogether, the 1968 Census reveals that there were twenty-three firms in the cast iron stoves and grates subdivision of the iron castings industry, while other firms in the iron castings industry, classified in other subdivisions, doubtless contributed sales. It would certainly be surprising if the leading five firms in the sector had 90 per cent or more of sales in 1958.

The above sifting process leaves us with two fairly firm candidates for consideration – primary batteries and accumulators. The accumulator product group has been dealt with by the Monopolies Commission,[3] and from figures given in that source it appears that the top five manufacturers accounted for just over 90 per cent of British-produced sales of accumulators in 1960 – and rather more if small firms with less than twenty-five employees are excluded from consideration.[4] The two leading manufacturers – Chloride Electrical Storage and Joseph Lucas, responsible for some 71 per cent of sales in 1960 – had both expanded by acquisition. Chloride acquired eleven companies over the period 1922–43, while Lucas had acquired the important concerns of C. A. Vandervell and Rotax (motor accessories) in 1926. The Monopolies Commission found a number of things against the public interest: Lucas's profits were excessive and against the public interest, while Chloride's profits were 'on the high side'; resale price maintenance was against the public interest, as was the agreement on the exchange of information maintained by the British Starter Battery Association.[5] The practice whereby prices of initial equipment and of replacement equipment were differentiated was against the public interest, and the

---

[1] In weight terms electrically powered iron castings appliances were 29·3 per cent of total iron castings output in the sector by 1958 according to *Iron and Steel Annual Statistics, 1958*, London, Iron and Steel Board, 1959.

[2] *Impending Structural Changes in the Domestic Electrical Appliances Industry*, London, Management Information, 1963, p. 8.

[3] *Report on the Supply of Electrical Equipment.*

[4] Ibid. paras. 6 and 376ff., and Customs and Excise, *Annual Statement of Trade of the United Kingdom, 1958*, London, HMSO, 1960.   [5] Ibid. para. 1055.

Commission deplored the fact that Chloride and Lucas had avoided competition with one another in the field of initial equipment.

These findings added up to a fairly round condemnation of monopolistic abuses in the product group. Whether publication of the findings has tended to curb abuses is another matter. The product group is expanding and encounters little import competition. The buyers of the product in the initial equipment sector are the car producers, and the production of cars is monopolised. Evely and Little considered that entry barriers to the trade were very high.[1]

Whether primary batteries had a five-firm sales concentration ratio of over 90 per cent in 1958 is less clear. The Prices and Incomes Board has reported on the product,[2] and the Monopolies Commission is now investigating it. Ever Ready was said by the Prices and Incomes Board to control over 70 per cent of sales of dry primary batteries, which make up the vast majority of sales. One firm, Mallory Batteries, in which Ever Ready has roughly one quarter of the equity interest, dominates the subsector in wet primary batteries. In fact, Ever Ready makes batteries for other distributors using their own brands, and its proportion of sales produced in the United Kingdom (imports were roughly 6 per cent of market supplies in 1969) is nearer 80 than 70 per cent. The broad drift of the Prices and Incomes Board version of Ever Ready's growth to dominance implies that acquisitions have played little part in its expansion. Speaking of the 1914–18 period it says: 'The war years stimulated technical development and the company's growth continued, partially by acquisition of other enterprises, but also by internal expansion and rationalisation of production.'[3] Since the 1939–45 period, the withdrawal of a number of large competitors meant that Ever Ready '. . . increased its share of a growing market in this country'.[4] The Annual Reports of Ever Ready reveal that three companies had been acquired by 1947 (Lissens, Vince's Dry Batteries, and Grosvenor Electric Batteries), of which the first was acquired for its interests in radio production and helped Ever Ready to expand into batteries for use in radios. The other two acquisitions were not large companies. None of the other important concerns in the sector appears to have grown by acquisition.[5]

There do not seem to be any significant constraints upon producers in this trade. Imports have less than 10 per cent of an expanding market and there are no large buyers of the product. Entry barriers appear to be significantly high. Brand loyalties and the comprehensive distribution system operated by Ever Ready,[6] as well as the costs of acquiring technical know-how, must be a deterrent to many potential entrants. Evely and Little judged that this trade was one

---

[1] *Concentration in British Industry*, p. 143.

[2] National Board for Prices and Incomes, *Report No. 148. Prices of Primary Batteries Proposed by the Ever Ready Company (Great Britain) Ltd*, Cmnd 4370, London, HMSO, 1970.

[3] Ibid. para. 11.

[4] Ibid. para. 12.

[5] Other important firms remaining after the atrophy of the post-1945 years were, in the late 1950s – AEI, which discontinued production in the early 1960s, Vidor, Ray-o-Vac International, Tungstone Products, Mallory Batteries, Ferguson and Le Carbone. The latter two concerns merged during the 1960s.

[6] The company services 90 per cent of potential outlets in the United Kingdom, '. . . the majority of them directly, by a van sales organisation operating from area depots' (ibid. para. 20).

where the incidence of obstacles to new entry and growth appeared to be most significant.[1]

In summary, this survey has shown that only two more products probably qualified for inclusion in chapters 3–6, but in accumulators high concentration was the result of external growth and in primary batteries it emerged mainly from Ever Ready's internal growth. Our conclusion about the role of external and internal growth in the emergence of high concentration is thus not affected.

It appears that a case could be made for adding both products to the list of those produced under unconstrained monopoly conditions which appears in the summary to chapter 6. But the trade in accumulators has been investigated by the Monopolies Commission, and the trade in primary batteries is currently being investigated.

Concentration in British Industry, p. 143.

INDEX OF COMPANIES

(Only companies which could be traced as still in existence in 1970–1, either independently or as subsidiaries, are included. The words 'Company' and 'Limited' are omitted from all the names.)

INDEX OF PRODUCTS AND TRADES

(Sub-products shown only in appendix A are not included)

INDEX OF AUTHORS

PUBLICATIONS OF THE
NATIONAL INSTITUTE OF ECONOMIC
AND SOCIAL RESEARCH

published by

THE CAMBRIDGE UNIVERSITY PRESS

Books published for the Institute by the Cambridge University Press are available through the ordinary booksellers. They appear in the five series below:

ECONOMIC & SOCIAL STUDIES

* At present out of print.

OCCASIONAL PAPERS

*At present out of print.

STUDIES IN THE NATIONAL INCOME AND EXPENDITURE OF THE UNITED KINDGOM

Published under the joint auspices of the National Institute and the Department of Applied Economics, Cambridge.

NIESR STUDENTS EDITION

*At present out of print.

REGIONAL PAPERS

1   *The Anatomy of Regional Activity Rates* by JOHN BOWERS, and *Regional Social Accounts for the United Kingdom* by V. H. WOODWARD. 1970. pp. 192. £1.25 net.

2   *Regional Unemployment Differences in Great Britain* by P. C. CHESHIRE and *Interregional Migration Models and their Application to Great Britain* by R. WEEDEN. 1973. pp. 118. £2.00 net.

THE NATIONAL INSTITUTE OF ECONOMIC AND SOCIAL RESEARCH

publishes regularly

THE NATIONAL INSTITUTE ECONOMIC REVIEW

A quarterly analysis of the general economic situation in the United Kingdom and the world overseas, with forecasts eighteen months ahead. The first issue each year is devoted entirely to the current situation and prospects both in the short and medium term. Other issues contain also special articles on subjects of interest to academic and business economists.

Annual subscriptions, £6.00, and single issues for the current year, £1.75 each, are available directly from NIESR, 2 Dean Trench Street, Smith Square, London, SW1P 3HE.

Subscriptions at the special reduced price of £2.50 p.a. are available to students in the United Kingdom and the Irish Republic on application to the Secretary of the Institute.

Back numbers, including reprints of those which have gone out of stock, are distributed by Wm. Dawson and Sons Ltd., Cannon House, Park Farm Road, Folkestone, price £2.00 each plus postage.

Also available directly from the Institute

THE IVTH FRENCH PLAN

By FRANCOIS PERROUX, translated by Bruno Leblanc. 1965. pp. 72. 50p net.

Published by Heinemann Educational Books

AN INCOMES POLICY FOR BRITAIN

Edited by FRANK BLACKABY. 1972. pp. 260. £4.00 net.

MEDIUM-TERM ASSESSMENTS OF THE BRITISH ECONOMY

Edited by G.D.N. WORSWICK and FRANK BLACKABY. 1974. pp. 268. £4.80 net.

Available from booksellers.